LITERATURE CONNECTIONS

The Tempest

and Related Readings

A HOUGHTON MIFFLIN COMPANY
Evanston, Illinois • Boston • Dallas

Acknowledgments

"The Tempest" and "Caliban," from *The Friendly Shakespeare* by Norrie Epstein. Copyright © 1993 by Norrie Epstein, Jon Winokur and Reid Boates. Used by permission of Viking Penguin, a division of Penguin Putnam Inc.

Excerpts from "True Reportory," from *A Voyage to Virginia in 1609* edited by Louis B. Wright. Copyright © 1964 by the Rector and Visitors of the University of Virginia. Reprinted with permission of the University Press of Virginia.

A Tempest by Aimé Césaire, translated by Richard Miller. English translation copyright © 1985 by Richard Miller. Originally published in French as *Une Tempête* by Editions du Seuil, Paris. Copyright © 1969 by Editions du Seuil. Reprinted by permission of Georges Borchardt, Inc.

"I Will Come Back," from *Pablo Neruda: Selected Poems* by Pablo Neruda, translated by Alastair Reid. Copyright © Pablo Neruda and Fundación Pablo Neruda. Copyright © 1970 by Anthony Kerrigan, W. S. Merwin, Alastair Reid and Nathaniel Tarn. Reprinted by permission of Agencia Literaria Carmen Balcells, S.A., and Jonathan Cape, Ltd., a division of Random House, UK.

Cover illustration by Michael Steirnagle.

Warning: No part of this work may be reproduced or transmitted in any form or by any means, electronic or mechanical, including photocopying and recording, or by any information storage or retrieval system without prior written permission of McDougal Littell Inc. unless such copying is expressly permitted by federal copyright law. With the exception of not-for-profit transcription in Braille, McDougal Littell Inc. is not authorized to grant permission for further uses of copyrighted selections reprinted in this text without the permission of their owners. Permission must be obtained from the individual copyright owners as identified herein. Address inquiries to Manager, Rights and Permissions, McDougal Littell Inc., P.O. Box 1667, Evanston, IL 60204.

ISBN 0-618-16122-8

Copyright © 2002 by McDougal Littell Inc. All rights reserved.
Printed in the United States of America.

1 2 3 4 5 6 7—DCI—05 04 03 02 01

Contents

The Tempest
A romance that explores love and hate, good and evil, fantasy and reality
play by William Shakespeare   3

The Tempest
What insights can we gather from Shakespeare's last play?
essay by Norrie Epstein   169

from *A True Reportory of the Wreck and Redemption of Sir Thomas Gates, Knight*
A witness attests to a disastrous storm.
historical account by William Strachey   176

The Sire de Malétroit's Door
What makes two people fall in love?
short story by Robert Louis Stevenson   181

Rappaccini's Daughter
Love baits an unsuspecting victim.
short story by Nathaniel Hawthorne   206

Caliban
A modern take on this unusual character
essay by Norrie Epstein   242

from *A Tempest*
  How do Prospero, Caliban, and Ariel really feel about each other?
  drama by Aimé Cesaire   245

I Will Come Back
  Leaving one's mark on the world
  poem by Pablo Neruda   251

The Tempest

William Shakespeare

The Scene: *A barren island in the Mediterranean Sea*

Characters

Prospero, the former duke of Milan, now a magician on a Mediterranean island

Miranda, Prospero's daughter

Ariel, a spirit, servant to Prospero

Caliban, an inhabitant of the island, servant to Prospero

Ferdinand, prince of Naples

Alonso, king of Naples

Antonio, duke of Milan and Prospero's brother

Sebastian, Alonso's brother

Gonzalo, councillor to Alonso and friend to Prospero

Adrian
Francisco } courtiers in attendance on Alonso

Trinculo, servant to Alonso

Stephano, Alonso's butler

Shipmaster

Boatswain

Mariners

Players who, as spirits, take the roles of **Iris, Ceres, Juno, Nymphs,** and **Reapers** in Prospero's masque, and who, in other scenes, take the roles of "islanders" and of hunting dogs

1 **Boatswain:** a low-ranking ship's officer (pronounced "bosun").
2 **What cheer?:** How goes it with you?
3 **Good:** good fellow; **Fall to 't yarely:** proceed quickly.
4 **Bestir:** get moving.

5 **hearts:** hearties; **Cheerly:** heartily.
6 **Tend:** pay attention.
7–8 **Blow . . . enough:** The storm can blow its hardest as long as we have enough room to sail safely.

10 **Play the men:** Act like men.

16–17 **What cares . . . king?:** What do these roaring waves care about a king's rank?

ACT ONE

Scene 1

[*A tempestuous noise of thunder and lightning heard. Enter a* Shipmaster *and a* Boatswain.]

Master. Boatswain!

Boatswain. Here, master. What cheer?

Master. Good, speak to th' mariners. Fall to 't yarely or we run ourselves aground. Bestir, bestir!

[*He exits.*]

[*Enter Mariners.*]

5 **Boatswain.** Heigh, my hearts! Cheerly, cheerly, my hearts! Yare, yare! Take in the topsail. Tend to th' Master's whistle.—Blow till thou burst thy wind, if room enough!

[*Enter* Alonso, Sebastian, Antonio, Ferdinand, Gonzalo, *and others.*]

Alonso. Good boatswain, have care. Where's the
10 Master? Play the men.

Boatswain. I pray now, keep below.

Antonio. Where is the Master, boatswain?

Boatswain. Do you not hear him? You mar our labor. Keep your cabins. You do assist the storm.

15 **Gonzalo.** Nay, good, be patient.

Boatswain. When the sea is. Hence! What cares these roarers for the name of king? To cabin! Silence! Trouble us not.

The Tempest   5

21 ***councillor:*** adviser or member of the king's council.
21–23 ***command . . . present:*** quiet the wind and waves and establish order.
23 ***hand:*** handle.

26 ***mischance of the hour:*** impending disaster; ***hap:*** happen.

29–30 An allusion to the proverb "He that is born to be hanged shall never be drowned." Many Elizabethans believed that moles can reveal how someone will die. *What do you think Gonzalo is suggesting about the boatswain with this allusion?*
32 ***cable:*** anchor cable; ***doth little advantage:*** is of little use.

35 ***Bring . . . course:*** Use the mainsail to bring the ship close to the wind (keep it away from the island by sailing at an angle into the wind).
36–37 ***They are . . . office:*** The passengers make more noise than the storm and us as we work.

38 ***give o'er:*** give up.

40 ***A pox o':*** a curse on.

6   **Literature Connections**

Gonzalo. Good, yet remember whom thou hast aboard.

Boatswain. None that I more love than myself. You are a councillor; if you can command these elements to silence, and work the peace of the present, we will not hand a rope more. Use your authority. If you cannot, give thanks you have lived so long, and make yourself ready in your cabin for the mischance of the hour, if it so hap.—Cheerly, good hearts!—Out of our way, I say!

[*He exits.*]

Gonzalo. I have great comfort from this fellow. Methinks he hath no drowning mark upon him. His complexion is perfect gallows. Stand fast, good Fate, to his hanging. Make the rope of his destiny our cable, for our own doth little advantage. If he be not born to be hanged, our case is miserable.

[*He exits with* Alonso, Sebastian, *and the other courtiers.*]

[*Enter* Boatswain.]

Boatswain. Down with the topmast! Yare! Lower, lower! Bring her to try wi' th' main course. [*a cry within*] A plague upon this howling! They are louder than the weather or our office.

[*Enter* Sebastian, Antonio, *and* Gonzalo.]

Yet again? What do you here? Shall we give o'er and drown? Have you a mind to sink?

Sebastian. A pox o' your throat, you bawling, blasphemous, incharitable dog!

Boatswain. Work you, then.

Antonio. Hang, cur, hang, you whoreson, insolent noisemaker! We are less afraid to be drowned than thou art.

46 *warrant him for:* guarantee him against; ***though:*** even if.

48 *unstanched wench:* unclean or immoral woman.

49 *Lay . . . courses:* Keep the ship close to the wind. Set the foresail and mainsail.

56 *merely:* utterly.

57 *wide-chopped:* bigmouthed.

57–58 Antonio exaggerates the traditional punishment for pirates, which was to hang them at the shore and leave their corpses until three tides had washed over them.

60 *gape . . . him:* open wide to swallow him.

64 *heath:* heather.

65 *furze:* a shrub.

66 *fain:* willingly.

Gonzalo. I'll warrant him for drowning, though the ship were no stronger than a nutshell and as leaky as an unstanched wench.

Boatswain. Lay her ahold, ahold! Set her two courses. Off to sea again! Lay her off!

[*Enter more* Mariners, *wet.*]

Mariners. All lost! To prayers, to prayers! All lost!

[Mariners *exit.*]

Boatswain. What, must our mouths be cold?

Gonzalo. The King and Prince at prayers. Let's assist them, for our case is as theirs.

Sebastian. I am out of patience.

Antonio. We are merely cheated of our lives by drunkards. This wide-chopped rascal—would thou mightst lie drowning the washing of ten tides!

[Boatswain *exits.*]

Gonzalo. He'll be hanged yet, though every drop of water swear against it and gape at wid'st to glut him.

[*A confused noise within:* "Mercy on us!"—"We split, we split!"—"Farewell, my wife and children!"—"Farewell, brother!"—"We split, we split, we split!"]

Antonio. Let's all sink wi' th' King.

Sebastian. Let's take leave of him.

[*He exits with* Antonio.]

Gonzalo. Now would I give a thousand furlongs of sea for an acre of barren ground: long heath, brown furze, anything. The wills above be done, but I would fain die a dry death.

[*He exits.*]

1 ***art:*** magic; skill.

3 ***pitch:*** a tarlike substance used for waterproofing ships.
4 ***welkin's:*** sky's.

6 ***brave:*** fine.

11 ***or ere:*** before.

13 ***fraughting souls:*** passengers.

14 ***amazement:*** bewilderment; ***piteous:*** compassionate.

18 ***naught knowing:*** knowing nothing.
19 ***whence I am:*** where I come from; ***more better:*** of higher rank.
20 ***full poor cell:*** very humble dwelling.

22 ***meddle with:*** enter.

Scene 2

[*Enter* Prospero *and* Miranda.]

Miranda. If by your art, my dearest father, you have
Put the wild waters in this roar, allay them.
The sky, it seems, would pour down stinking pitch,
But that the sea, mounting to th' welkin's cheek,
5 Dashes the fire out. O, I have suffered
With those that I saw suffer! A brave vessel,
Who had, no doubt, some noble creature in her,
Dashed all to pieces. O, the cry did knock
Against my very heart! Poor souls, they perished.
10 Had I been any god of power, I would
Have sunk the sea within the earth or ere
It should the good ship so have swallowed, and
The fraughting souls within her.

Prospero.   Be collected.
No more amazement. Tell your piteous heart
15 There's no harm done.

Miranda.   O, woe the day!

Prospero.   No harm.
I have done nothing but in care of thee,
Of thee, my dear one, thee, my daughter, who
Art ignorant of what thou art, naught knowing
Of whence I am, nor that I am more better
20 Than Prospero, master of a full poor cell,
And thy no greater father.

Miranda.   More to know
Did never meddle with my thoughts.

Prospero.   'Tis time
I should inform thee farther. Lend thy hand
And pluck my magic garment from me.

[*putting aside his cloak*]

                                       So,

26 ***direful spectacle:*** terrible display.
27 ***virtue:*** essence.
28 ***provision:*** foresight.

30 ***perdition:*** loss.
31 ***Betid:*** happened.

35 ***bootless inquisition:*** useless inquiry.

37 ***ope:*** open.

41 ***Out:*** fully.

43 ***Of anything . . . me:*** describe to me anything.

45–46 ***an assurance . . . warrants:*** a certainty that my memory guarantees to be true.

50 ***backward:*** past; ***abysm:*** abyss.
51 ***aught ere:*** anything before.

25   Lie there, my art.—Wipe thou thine eyes. Have comfort.
      The direful spectacle of the wrack, which touched
      The very virtue of compassion in thee,
      I have with such provision in mine art
      So safely ordered that there is no soul—
30   No, not so much perdition as an hair,
      Betid to any creature in the vessel
      Which thou heard'st cry, which thou saw'st sink. Sit down,
      For thou must now know farther.

   [*They sit.*]

   Miranda.   You have often
      Begun to tell me what I am, but stopped
35   And left me to a bootless inquisition,
      Concluding "Stay. Not yet."

   Prospero.   The hour's now come.
      The very minute bids thee ope thine ear.
      Obey, and be attentive. Canst thou remember
      A time before we came unto this cell?
40   I do not think thou canst, for then thou wast not
      Out three years old.

   Miranda.   Certainly, sir, I can.

   Prospero. By what? By any other house or person?
      Of anything the image tell me that
      Hath kept with thy remembrance.

   Miranda.   'Tis far off
45   And rather like a dream than an assurance
      That my remembrance warrants. Had I not
      Four or five women once that tended me?

   Prospero. Thou hadst, and more, Miranda. But how is it
      That this lives in thy mind? What seest thou else
50   In the dark backward and abysm of time?
      If thou rememb'rest aught ere thou cam'st here,
      How thou cam'st here thou mayst.

The Tempest

53 ***Twelve year since:*** twelve years ago.

56 ***piece of virtue:*** model of chastity.

59 ***no worse issued:*** no less nobly born.

63 ***holp hither:*** helped here.

64 ***o' th' teen:*** of the trouble.
65 ***from:*** absent from.

68 ***perfidious:*** treacherous; ***next:*** next to.

70 ***manage:*** administration; ***state:*** dukedom.
71 ***signories:*** lordships; ***first:*** foremost.
72 ***prime:*** most important.

76 ***grew stranger:*** became remote; ***transported:*** carried away.
77 ***rapt:*** engrossed.
78 ***attend:*** pay attention to.

79 ***Being once perfected:*** having mastered; ***suits:*** petitions.

Miranda. But that I do not.

Prospero. Twelve year since, Miranda, twelve year since,
Thy father was the Duke of Milan and
A prince of power.

Miranda. Sir, are not you my father?

Prospero. Thy mother was a piece of virtue, and
She said thou wast my daughter. And thy father
Was Duke of Milan, and his only heir
And princess no worse issued.

Miranda. O, the heavens!
What foul play had we that we came from thence?
Or blessèd was 't we did?

Prospero. Both, both, my girl.
By foul play, as thou sayst, were we heaved thence,
But blessedly holp hither.

Miranda. O, my heart bleeds
To think o' th' teen that I have turned you to,
Which is from my remembrance. Please you, farther.

Prospero. My brother and thy uncle, called Antonio—
I pray thee, mark me—that a brother should
Be so perfidious!—he whom next thyself
Of all the world I loved, and to him put
The manage of my state, as at that time
Through all the signories it was the first,
And Prospero the prime duke, being so reputed
In dignity, and for the liberal arts
Without a parallel. Those being all my study,
The government I cast upon my brother
And to my state grew stranger, being transported
And rapt in secret studies. Thy false uncle—
Dost thou attend me?

Miranda. Sir, most heedfully.

Prospero. Being once perfected how to grant suits,
How to deny them, who t' advance, and who

The Tempest 15

81 **trash:** restrain; **overtopping:** exceeding their authority.
82 **creatures:** officials who owe their position to a patron.
82–83 **or changed . . . formed 'em:** either changed their allegiance or created new officials.

85 **that:** so that.

87 **verdure:** sap; vitality.

90 **closeness:** privacy.
91–92 **but by . . . rate:** was more valuable than the public could appreciate merely because it was so secluded.

94 **did beget of him:** fathered or produced in him.

97 **sans bound:** without limit.
97–105 **He being . . . prerogative:** With my revenue and whatever else my authority might command, Antonio was able to act like a lord; and like someone who has told a lie so often that he mistakes it for truth, he came to believe that he was really the duke, as a consequence of taking over my role and appearing to have all the privileges of royalty.

108–110 **To have . . . Milan:** To have no barrier between himself and his role, he must become the duke of Milan without any restrictions.
110 **Me:** for me.
111 **temporal royalties:** worldly powers.
112–117 **confederates . . . stooping:** Antonio was so thirsty for power that he formed an alliance with the king of Naples, agreeing to make annual payments, to declare his obedience, and to turn Milan into a subject state. (A coronet is a crown worn by a nobleman rather than a king.)

To trash for overtopping, new created
The creatures that were mine, I say, or changed 'em,
Or else new formed 'em, having both the key
Of officer and office, set all hearts i' th' state
To what tune pleased his ear, that now he was
The ivy which had hid my princely trunk
And sucked my verdure out on 't. Thou attend'st not.

Miranda. O, good sir, I do.

Prospero.   I pray thee, mark me.
I, thus neglecting worldly ends, all dedicated
To closeness and the bettering of my mind
With that which, but by being so retired,
O'erprized all popular rate, in my false brother
Awaked an evil nature, and my trust,
Like a good parent, did beget of him
A falsehood in its contrary as great
As my trust was, which had indeed no limit,
A confidence sans bound. He being thus lorded,
Not only with what my revenue yielded
But what my power might else exact, like one
Who, having into truth by telling of it,
Made such a sinner of his memory
To credit his own lie, he did believe
He was indeed the Duke, out o' th' substitution
And executing th' outward face of royalty
With all prerogative. Hence, his ambition growing—
Dost thou hear?

Miranda. Your tale, sir, would cure deafness.

Prospero. To have no screen between this part he played
And him he played it for, he needs will be
Absolute Milan. Me, poor man, my library
Was dukedom large enough. Of temporal royalties
He thinks me now incapable; confederates,
So dry he was for sway, wi' th' King of Naples
To give him annual tribute, do him homage,
Subject his coronet to his crown, and bend

118 ***his condition:*** the terms of his agreement; ***event:*** outcome.

123 ***hearkens . . . suit:*** listens to my brother's proposal.
124–128 ***in lieu . . . brother:*** In return for Antonio's agreement to pay homage and tribute, the king of Naples was to immediately remove Prospero and his family from Milan and give the dukedom to Antonio.

132 ***ministers:*** agents.

135 ***hint:*** occasion.

139 ***impertinent:*** irrelevant; ***Wherefore:*** why.

141 ***durst:*** dared.

    The dukedom, yet unbowed—alas, poor Milan!—
    To most ignoble stooping.

Miranda.   O, the heavens!

Prospero. Mark his condition and th' event. Then tell me
    If this might be a brother.

Miranda.   I should sin
120   To think but nobly of my grandmother.
    Good wombs have borne bad sons.

Prospero.   Now the condition.
    This King of Naples, being an enemy
    To me inveterate, hearkens my brother's suit,
    Which was that he, in lieu o' th' premises
125   Of homage and I know not how much tribute,
    Should presently extirpate me and mine
    Out of the dukedom, and confer fair Milan,
    With all the honors, on my brother; whereon,
    A treacherous army levied, one midnight
130   Fated to th' purpose did Antonio open
    The gates of Milan, and i' th' dead of darkness
    The ministers for th' purpose hurried thence
    Me and thy crying self.

Miranda.   Alack, for pity!
    I, not rememb'ring how I cried out then,
135   Will cry it o'er again. It is a hint
    That wrings mine eyes to 't.

Prospero.   Hear a little further,
    And then I'll bring thee to the present business
    Which now 's upon 's, without the which this story
    Were most impertinent.

Miranda.   Wherefore did they not
140   That hour destroy us?

Prospero.   Well demanded, wench.
    My tale provokes that question. Dear, they durst not,
    So dear the love my people bore me, nor set

145 *few:* brief; ***bark:*** ship.

147 ***butt:*** barrel or tub.
148 ***Nor . . . nor:*** having neither . . . nor.

151–152 ***sighing back . . . wrong:*** the wind's sympathetic sighing wronged us by blowing the boat out to sea. *What does this description suggest about Prospero's vision of nature?*

156 ***decked:*** adorned.
157–158 ***which raised . . . bear up:*** your smiling gave me the courage to endure.

166 ***stuffs:*** materials.
167 ***have steaded much:*** have been very useful; ***gentleness:*** nobility.

        A mark so bloody on the business, but
        With colors fairer painted their foul ends.
145   In few, they hurried us aboard a bark,
        Bore us some leagues to sea, where they prepared
        A rotten carcass of a butt, not rigged,
        Nor tackle, sail, nor mast; the very rats
        Instinctively have quit it. There they hoist us
150   To cry to th' sea that roared to us, to sigh
        To th' winds, whose pity, sighing back again,
        Did us but loving wrong.

Miranda.   Alack, what trouble
    Was I then to you!

Prospero.   O, a cherubin
    Thou wast that did preserve me. Thou didst smile,
155 Infusèd with a fortitude from heaven,
    When I have decked the sea with drops full salt,
    Under my burden groaned, which raised in me
    An undergoing stomach to bear up
    Against what should ensue.

160 **Miranda.** How came we ashore?

Prospero. By providence divine.
    Some food we had, and some fresh water, that
    A noble Neapolitan, Gonzalo,
    Out of his charity, who being then appointed
165 Master of this design, did give us, with
    Rich garments, linens, stuffs, and necessaries,
    Which since have steaded much. So, of his gentleness,
    Knowing I loved my books, he furnished me
    From mine own library with volumes that
170 I prize above my dukedom.

Miranda.   Would I might
    But ever see that man.

Prospero [*standing*].   Now I arise.
    Sit still, and hear the last of our sea-sorrow.
    Here in this island we arrived, and here

174 *made thee more profit:* made you profit more.
175 *princes:* royal children.

181 *Now my dear lady:* now on my side. (Fortune was often personified as a fickle woman.)
183 *my zenith:* the high point of my fortunes.

185 *omit:* fail to take advantage of.

187 *dullness:* drowsiness.

195 *quality:* abilities or fellow spirits.

196 *to point:* in exact detail.

198 *beak:* prow.
199 *waist:* middle part of a ship; *deck:* poop deck (at the stern).
200 *flamed amazement:* caused terror by appearing as a flame. (The effect is similar to a phenomenon called St. Elmo's fire, which can occur on ships during electrical storms.)

  Have I, thy schoolmaster, made thee more profit
175 Than other princes can, that have more time
  For vainer hours and tutors not so careful.

 Miranda. Heavens thank you for 't. And now I pray
   you, sir—
  For still 'tis beating in my mind—your reason
  For raising this sea storm?

 Prospero.   Know thus far forth:
180 By accident most strange, bountiful Fortune,
  Now my dear lady, hath mine enemies
  Brought to this shore; and by my prescience
  I find my zenith doth depend upon
  A most auspicious star, whose influence
185 If now I court not, but omit, my fortunes
  Will ever after droop. Here cease more questions.
  Thou art inclined to sleep. 'Tis a good dullness,
  And give it way. I know thou canst not choose.

[Miranda *falls asleep.* Prospero *puts on his cloak.*]

  Come away, servant, come. I am ready now.
190 Approach, my Ariel. Come.

[*Enter* Ariel.]

 Ariel. All hail, great master! Grave sir, hail! I come
  To answer thy best pleasure. Be 't to fly,
  To swim, to dive into the fire, to ride
  On the curled clouds, to thy strong bidding task
195 Ariel and all his quality.

 Prospero.   Hast thou, spirit,
  Performed to point the tempest that I bade thee?

 Ariel. To every article.
  I boarded the King's ship; now on the beak,
  Now in the waist, the deck, in every cabin,
200 I flamed amazement. Sometimes I'd divide
  And burn in many places. On the topmast,
  The yards, and bowsprit would I flame distinctly,

205 *sight-outrunning:* quicker than the eye.
206–208 *Neptune:* god of the sea (who carries a **trident,** or three-pronged spear).

209 *coil:* turmoil.

211 *of the mad:* such as madmen feel.
212 *tricks of desperation:* desperate actions.

215 *up-staring:* standing on end.

218 *nigh:* near.

220 *sustaining garments:* garments that helped them float.
221 *bad'st:* commanded.
222 *troops:* groups.

225 *odd angle:* out-of-the-way corner.

　　　　　　Then meet and join. Jove's lightning, the precursors
　　　　　　O' th' dreadful thunderclaps, more momentary
205　　　　And sight-outrunning were not. The fire and cracks
　　　　　　Of sulfurous roaring the most mighty Neptune
　　　　　　Seem to besiege and make his bold waves tremble,
　　　　　　Yea, his dread trident shake.

　　　　Prospero.　　　　　　　　　My brave spirit!
　　　　　　Who was so firm, so constant, that this coil
210　　　　Would not infect his reason?

　　　　Ariel.　　　　　　　　　　Not a soul
　　　　　　But felt a fever of the mad, and played
　　　　　　Some tricks of desperation. All but mariners
　　　　　　Plunged in the foaming brine and quit the vessel,
　　　　　　Then all afire with me. The King's son, Ferdinand,
215　　　　With hair up-staring—then like reeds, not hair—
　　　　　　Was the first man that leaped; cried "Hell is empty,
　　　　　　And all the devils are here."

　　　　Prospero.　　　　　　　　Why, that's my spirit!
　　　　　　But was not this nigh shore?

　　　　Ariel.　　　　　　　　　　Close by, my master.

　　　　Prospero. But are they, Ariel, safe?

　　　　Ariel.　　　　　　　　　　Not a hair perished.
220　　　　On their sustaining garments not a blemish,
　　　　　　But fresher than before; and, as thou bad'st me,
　　　　　　In troops I have dispersed them 'bout the isle.
　　　　　　The King's son have I landed by himself,
　　　　　　Whom I left cooling of the air with sighs
225　　　　In an odd angle of the isle, and sitting,
　　　　　　His arms in this sad knot.

　　　　[*He folds his arms.*]

　　　　Prospero.　　　　　　　　Of the King's ship,
　　　　　　The mariners say how thou hast disposed,
　　　　　　And all the rest o' th' fleet.

231 *still vexed Bermoothes:* always stormy Bermudas.

233 *with a . . . labor:* under the combined effects of my spell and their exhaustion.

236 *float:* sea.

241 *mid season:* noon.

242 *two glasses:* two o'clock (two hourglasses past noon).

244 *pains:* tasks.
245 *remember:* remind.

248 *prithee:* beg of you.

251 *or . . . or:* either . . . or.
252 *bate me:* deduct from the time of my service.

Ariel. Safely in harbor
Is the King's ship. In the deep nook, where once
Thou called'st me up at midnight to fetch dew
From the still-vexed Bermoothes, there she's hid;
The mariners all under hatches stowed,
Who, with a charm joined to their suffered labor,
I have left asleep. And for the rest o' th' fleet,
Which I dispersed, they all have met again
And are upon the Mediterranean float,
Bound sadly home for Naples,
Supposing that they saw the King's ship wracked
And his great person perish.

Prospero. Ariel, thy charge
Exactly is performed. But there's more work.
What is the time o' th' day?

Ariel. Past the mid season.

Prospero. At least two glasses. The time 'twixt six and now
Must by us both be spent most preciously.

Ariel. Is there more toil? Since thou dost give me pains,
Let me remember thee what thou hast promised,
Which is not yet performed me.

Prospero. How now? Moody?
What is 't thou canst demand?

Ariel. My liberty.

Prospero. Before the time be out? No more.

Ariel. I prithee,
Remember I have done thee worthy service,
Told thee no lies, made no mistakings, served
Without or grudge or grumblings. Thou did promise
To bate me a full year.

Prospero. Dost thou forget
From what a torment I did free thee?

257 **veins o' th' earth:** mineral veins or underground streams.
258 **baked:** hardened.

261 **grown into a hoop:** bent over.

264 **Argier:** Algiers.

269–272 Sycorax was exiled rather than killed, probably because she was pregnant (blue eyelids were thought to be a sign of pregnancy).

275 **for:** because.

277 **hests:** commands.
278 **ministers:** agents.

Ariel. No.

Prospero. Thou dost, and think'st it much to tread the ooze
255 Of the salt deep,
To run upon the sharp wind of the north,
To do me business in the veins o' th' earth
When it is baked with frost.

Ariel. I do not, sir.

Prospero. Thou liest, malignant thing. Hast thou forgot
260 The foul witch Sycorax, who with age and envy
Was grown into a hoop? Hast thou forgot her?

Ariel. No, sir.

Prospero. Thou hast. Where was she born? Speak. Tell me.

Ariel. Sir, in Argier.

Prospero. O, was she so? I must
265 Once in a month recount what thou hast been,
Which thou forget'st. This damned witch Sycorax,
For mischiefs manifold, and sorceries terrible
To enter human hearing, from Argier,
Thou know'st, was banished. For one thing she did
270 They would not take her life. Is not this true?

Ariel. Ay, sir.

Prospero. This blue-eyed hag was hither brought with child
And here was left by th' sailors. Thou, my slave,
As thou report'st thyself, was then her servant,
275 And for thou wast a spirit too delicate
To act her earthy and abhorred commands,
Refusing her grand hests, she did confine thee,
By help of her more potent ministers
And in her most unmitigable rage,
280 Into a cloven pine, within which rift
Imprisoned thou didst painfully remain

284 ***as mill wheels strike:*** as the blades of mill wheels strike the water.
285 ***litter:*** give birth to.

291 ***penetrate the breasts:*** arouse the sympathy.

300 ***correspondent:*** obedient.
301 ***spriting:*** spiriting; ***gently:*** willingly.

> A dozen years; within which space she died
> And left thee there, where thou didst vent thy groans
> As fast as mill wheels strike. Then was this island
> (Save for the son that she did litter here,
> A freckled whelp, hag-born) not honored with
> A human shape.

Ariel. Yes, Caliban, her son.

Prospero. Dull thing, I say so; he, that Caliban
> Whom now I keep in service. Thou best know'st
> What torment I did find thee in. Thy groans
> Did make wolves howl, and penetrate the breasts
> Of ever-angry bears. It was a torment
> To lay upon the damned, which Sycorax
> Could not again undo. It was mine art,
> When I arrived and heard thee, that made gape
> The pine and let thee out.

Ariel. I thank thee, master.

Prospero. If thou more murmur'st, I will rend an oak
> And peg thee in his knotty entrails till
> Thou hast howled away twelve winters.

Ariel. Pardon, master.
> I will be correspondent to command
> And do my spriting gently.

Prospero. Do so, and after two days
> I will discharge thee.

Ariel. That's my noble master.
> What shall I do? Say, what? What shall I do?

Prospero. Go make thyself like a nymph o' th' sea.
> Be subject
> To no sight but thine and mine, invisible
> To every eyeball else. Go, take this shape,
> And hither come in 't. Go, hence with diligence!

[*Ariel exits.*]

311 Heaviness: drowsiness.

315 miss: do without.
316 serves in offices: performs duties.

321 quaint: ingenious; elegant.

323 got: fathered.

324 dam: mother.

326 fen: bog.

Awake, dear heart, awake. Thou hast slept well.
Awake.

[Miranda *wakes*.]

Miranda. The strangeness of your story put
Heaviness in me.

Prospero. Shake it off. Come on,
We'll visit Caliban, my slave, who never
Yields us kind answer.

Miranda [*rising*]. 'Tis a villain, sir,
I do not love to look on.

Prospero. But, as 'tis,
We cannot miss him. He does make our fire,
Fetch in our wood, and serves in offices
That profit us.—What ho, slave, Caliban!
Thou earth, thou, speak!

Caliban [*within*]. There's wood enough within.

Prospero. Come forth, I say. There's other business
for thee.
Come, thou tortoise. When?

[*Enter* Ariel *like a water nymph*.]

Fine apparition! My quaint Ariel,
Hark in thine ear.

[*He whispers to* Ariel.]

Ariel. My lord, it shall be done.

[*He exits*.]

Prospero [*to* Caliban]. Thou poisonous slave, got by the devil himself
Upon thy wicked dam, come forth!

[*Enter* Caliban.]

Caliban. As wicked dew as e'er my mother brushed
With raven's feather from unwholesome fen

327 ***southwest:*** Winds from the southwest were considered unhealthy.

330 ***Urchins:*** hedgehogs or goblins.
331 ***forth at vast:*** go forth during the long stretch.
332–333 ***Thou shalt . . . honeycomb:*** The pinches on your body will be as dense as the cells in a honeycomb.

337 ***strok'st:*** stroked.

339 ***bigger light:*** the sun; ***the less:*** the moon.

343 ***charms:*** spells.

346 ***sty me:*** pen me up like a pig.

349 ***stripes:*** lashes; ***used:*** treated.

354 ***I had peopled else:*** otherwise I would have populated.

356 ***Which any . . . take:*** upon whom goodness cannot make any impression.

       Drop on you both. A southwest blow on you
       And blister you all o'er.

Prospero. For this, be sure, tonight thou shalt have cramps,
330   Side-stitches that shall pen thy breath up. Urchins
       Shall forth at vast of night that they may work
       All exercise on thee. Thou shalt be pinched
       As thick as honeycomb, each pinch more stinging
       Than bees that made 'em.

Caliban.   I must eat my dinner.
335   This island's mine by Sycorax, my mother,
       Which thou tak'st from me. When thou cam'st first,
       Thou strok'st me and made much of me, wouldst give me
       Water with berries in 't, and teach me how
       To name the bigger light and how the less,
340   That burn by day and night. And then I loved thee,
       And showed thee all the qualities o' th' isle,
       The fresh springs, brine pits, barren place and fertile.
       Cursed be I that did so! All the charms
       Of Sycorax, toads, beetles, bats, light on you,
345   For I am all the subjects that you have,
       Which first was mine own king; and here you sty me
       In this hard rock, whiles you do keep from me
       The rest o' th' island.

Prospero.   Thou most lying slave,
       Whom stripes may move, not kindness, I have used thee,
350   Filth as thou art, with humane care, and lodged thee
       In mine own cell, till thou didst seek to violate
       The honor of my child.

Caliban. O ho, O ho! Would 't had been done!
       Thou didst prevent me. I had peopled else
355   This isle with Calibans.

Miranda.   Abhorrèd slave,
       Which any print of goodness wilt not take,

357 *capable of all ill:* inclined to every evil.

362 *race:* natural disposition.

368 *red plague:* plague that causes red sores; ***rid:*** destroy.

369 *Hagseed:* witch's offspring.

371 *answer other business:* perform other tasks.

373 *rack . . . cramps:* torture you with the cramps of old people.

377 *Setebos:* a god that was worshiped in Patagonia, a region of South America.
378 *vassal:* servant or slave.

382 *whist:* into silence.

Being capable of all ill! I pitied thee,
Took pains to make thee speak, taught thee each hour
One thing or other. When thou didst not, savage,
Know thine own meaning, but wouldst gabble like
A thing most brutish, I endowed thy purposes
With words that made them known. But thy vile race,
Though thou didst learn, had that in 't which
    good natures
Could not abide to be with. Therefore wast thou
Deservedly confined into this rock,
Who hadst deserved more than a prison.

Caliban. You taught me language, and my profit on 't
Is I know how to curse. The red plague rid you
For learning me your language!

Prospero.   Hagseed, hence!
Fetch us in fuel; and be quick, thou 'rt best,
To answer other business. Shrugg'st thou, malice?
If thou neglect'st or dost unwillingly
What I command, I'll rack thee with old cramps,
Fill all thy bones with aches, make thee roar
That beasts shall tremble at thy din.

Caliban.   No, pray thee.
[*aside*] I must obey. His art is of such power
It would control my dam's god, Setebos,
And make a vassal of him.

Prospero.   So, slave, hence.

[Caliban *exits.*]

[*Enter* Ferdinand; *and* Ariel, *invisible, playing and singing.*]

[*song*]

Ariel.
Come unto these yellow sands,
    And then take hands.
Curtsied when you have, and kissed
    The wild waves whist.

383 ***Foot it featly:*** dance nimbly.
384–385 ***bear . . . burden:*** sing the refrain.

390 ***strain:*** tune; ***chanticleer:*** a rooster.

393 ***waits:*** attends.

397 ***passion:*** sorrow; suffering.
398 ***air:*** melody.

401 ***Full fathom five:*** fully five fathoms (30 feet) deep.

407 ***knell:*** funeral bell.

410 ***ditty:*** song; ***remember:*** commemorate.
411 ***mortal:*** human.

412 ***owes:*** owns.

>   *Foot it featly here and there,*
>   *And sweet sprites bear*
> 385   *The burden. Hark, hark!*
>   [*burden dispersedly, within:*] *Bow-wow.*
>   *The watchdogs bark.*
>   [*burden dispersedly, within:*] *Bow-wow.*
>   *Hark, hark! I hear*
> 390   *The strain of strutting chanticleer*
>   *Cry cock-a-diddle-dow.*

Ferdinand. Where should this music be? I' th' air, or
    th' earth?
It sounds no more; and sure it waits upon
Some god o' th' island. Sitting on a bank,
395 Weeping again the King my father's wrack,
This music crept by me upon the waters,
Allaying both their fury and my passion
With its sweet air. Thence I have followed it,
Or it hath drawn me rather. But 'tis gone.
400 No, it begins again.

[*song*]

Ariel.
> *Full fathom five thy father lies.*
>   *Of his bones are coral made.*
> *Those are pearls that were his eyes.*
>   *Nothing of him that doth fade*
> 405 *But doth suffer a sea change*
> *Into something rich and strange.*
>   *Sea nymphs hourly ring his knell.*
> [*burden, within:*] *Ding dong.*
>   *Hark, now I hear them: ding dong bell.*

410 **Ferdinand.** The ditty does remember my drowned
    father.
This is no mortal business, nor no sound
That the earth owes. I hear it now above me.

413 *fringèd curtains:* eyelids; *advance:* raise.

416 *brave form:* splendid appearance.

418 *gallant:* fine gentleman.
419 *but:* except that; *something:* somewhat.
420 *canker:* infection; spreading sore.

424 *It goes on:* my plan proceeds.

427 *Vouchsafe:* grant.
428 *May know:* that I may know; *remain:* dwell.

430 *bear me:* conduct myself.

432 *maid:* a girl (as opposed to a supernatural being).

434 *the best:* highest in rank.

Prospero [*to* Miranda]. The fringèd curtains of thine
    eye advance
And say what thou seest yond.

Miranda.   What is 't? A spirit?
415   Lord, how it looks about! Believe me, sir,
It carries a brave form. But 'tis a spirit.

Prospero. No, wench, it eats and sleeps and hath
    such senses
As we have, such. This gallant which thou seest
Was in the wrack; and, but he's something stained
420   With grief—that's beauty's canker—thou might'st
    call him
A goodly person. He hath lost his fellows
And strays about to find 'em.

Miranda.   I might call him
A thing divine, for nothing natural
I ever saw so noble.

Prospero [*aside*].   It goes on, I see,
425   As my soul prompts it. [*to* Ariel] Spirit, fine spirit,
    I'll free thee
Within two days for this.

Ferdinand [*seeing* Miranda]. Most sure, the goddess
On whom these airs attend!—Vouchsafe my prayer
May know if you remain upon this island,
And that you will some good instruction give
430   How I may bear me here. My prime request,
Which I do last pronounce, is—O you wonder!—
If you be maid or no.

Miranda.   No wonder, sir,
But certainly a maid.

Ferdinand.   My language! Heavens!
I am the best of them that speak this speech,
435   Were I but where 'tis spoken.

437 ***a single thing:*** one and the same. *What assumption has Ferdinand made about his father?*
438 ***Naples:*** king of Naples.

440 ***at ebb:*** dry.

443 ***twain:*** two.

444 ***control:*** refute.

446 ***changed eyes:*** exchanged loving looks.

448 ***done yourself some wrong:*** spoken in error.

453 ***your affection not gone forth:*** not already in love with someone else.

454 ***Soft:*** wait a minute.
455 ***either's:*** each other's.

456 ***uneasy:*** difficult; ***light:*** easy.
457 ***light:*** cheap.

458–459 ***Thou dost . . . not:*** You are unlawfully claiming the title of king, which is not rightly yours. *Why do you think Prospero makes this accusation?*

Prospero. How? The best?
What wert thou if the King of Naples heard thee?

Ferdinand. A single thing, as I am now, that wonders
To hear thee speak of Naples. He does hear me,
And that he does I weep. Myself am Naples,
440 Who with mine eyes, never since at ebb, beheld
The King my father wracked.

Miranda. Alack, for mercy!

Ferdinand. Yes, faith, and all his lords, the Duke of Milan
And his brave son being twain.

Prospero [*aside*]. The Duke of Milan
And his more braver daughter could control thee,
445 If now 'twere fit to do 't. At the first sight
They have changed eyes.—Delicate Ariel,
I'll set thee free for this. [*to* Ferdinand] A word, good sir.
I fear you have done yourself some wrong. A word.

Miranda. Why speaks my father so ungently? This
450 Is the third man that e'er I saw, the first
That e'er I sighed for. Pity move my father
To be inclined my way.

Ferdinand. O, if a virgin,
And your affection not gone forth, I'll make you
The Queen of Naples.

Prospero. Soft, sir, one word more.
455 [*aside*] They are both in either's powers. But this swift business
I must uneasy make, lest too light winning
Make the prize light. [*to* Ferdinand] One word more. I charge thee
That thou attend me. Thou dost here usurp
The name thou ow'st not, and hast put thyself
460 Upon this island as a spy, to win it
From me, the lord on 't.

462 ***such a temple:*** Antonio's handsome exterior.

468 ***fresh-brook mussels:*** freshwater mussels (which are inedible).

470 ***entertainment:*** treatment.

Stage direction—*charmed from moving:* put under a spell that immobilizes him.

472 ***rash a trial:*** strong a test.
473 ***gentle:*** noble.

474 ***My foot my tutor:*** should I let my inferior (Miranda) teach me how to act?

476 ***ward:*** fencer's defensive posture.
477 ***stick:*** magician's staff.

480 ***his surety:*** responsible for him.

Ferdinand. No, as I am a man!

Miranda. There's nothing ill can dwell in such a temple.
If the ill spirit have so fair a house,
Good things will strive to dwell with 't.

Prospero [*to* Ferdinand]. Follow me.
[*to* Miranda] Speak not you for him. He's a traitor.
  [*to* Ferdinand] Come,
I'll manacle thy neck and feet together.
Sea water shalt thou drink. Thy food shall be
The fresh-brook mussels, withered roots, and husks
Wherein the acorn cradled. Follow.

Ferdinand. No,
I will resist such entertainment till
Mine enemy has more power.

[*He draws, and is charmed from moving.*]

Miranda. O dear father,
Make not too rash a trial of him, for
He's gentle and not fearful.

Prospero. What, I say,
My foot my tutor?—Put thy sword up, traitor,
Who mak'st a show, but dar'st not strike, thy conscience
Is so possessed with guilt. Come from thy ward,
For I can here disarm thee with this stick
And make thy weapon drop.

Miranda. Beseech you, father—

Prospero. Hence! Hang not on my garments.

Miranda. Sir, have pity.
I'll be his surety.

Prospero. Silence! One word more
Shall make me chide thee, if not hate thee. What,
An advocate for an impostor? Hush.
Thou think'st there is no more such shapes as he,

485 *To:* compared to.

489 *Thy nerves . . . again:* your sinews are like those of a baby.

494 *but light:* of little importance.

496 *All corners else:* all other places.

502 *unwonted:* unusual.

504 *then:* if that is to occur.

                    Having seen but him and Caliban. Foolish wench,
485   To th' most of men this is a Caliban,
                    And they to him are angels.

            Miranda.   My affections
                    Are then most humble. I have no ambition
                    To see a goodlier man.

            Prospero [*to* Ferdinand].   Come on, obey.
                    Thy nerves are in their infancy again
490   And have no vigor in them.

            Ferdinand.   So they are.
                    My spirits, as in a dream, are all bound up.
                    My father's loss, the weakness which I feel,
                    The wrack of all my friends, nor this man's threats
                    To whom I am subdued, are but light to me,
495   Might I but through my prison once a day
                    Behold this maid. All corners else o' th' earth
                    Let liberty make use of. Space enough
                    Have I in such a prison.

            Prospero [*aside*].   It works.—Come on.—
                    Thou hast done well, fine Ariel.—Follow me.
500   [*to* Ariel] Hark what thou else shalt do me.

            Miranda [*to* Ferdinand].   Be of comfort.
                    My father's of a better nature, sir,
                    Than he appears by speech. This is unwonted
                    Which now came from him.

            Prospero [*to* Ariel].   Thou shalt be as free
                    As mountain winds; but then exactly do
505   All points of my command.

            Ariel.   To th' syllable.

            Prospero [*to* Ferdinand]. Come follow. [*to* Miranda]
                    Speak not for him.

            [*They exit.*]

3 ***beyond:*** greater than; ***hint:*** occasion.

5 ***The masters . . . the merchant:*** the officers or owners of some merchant ship and the merchant who owns the cargo.
6 ***just:*** exactly.

11 ***cold porridge:*** pease porridge (a pun on Alonso's cry for "peace").
12 ***visitor:*** a person responsible for comforting the sick in their homes; ***give him o'er so:*** abandon him.

16 ***One:*** It has struck one; ***Tell:*** Keep count. *What attitude do Sebastian and Antonio seem to have toward Gonzalo?*
17 ***entertained:*** held in the mind.
18 ***entertainer:*** person who holds the grief.

19 ***A dollar:*** a pun on the meaning of *entertainer* as "someone who is paid to amuse others."
20 ***Dolor:*** sorrow. This is a play on the word *dollar* in line 19.

ACT TWO

Scene 1

[*Enter* Alonso, Sebastian, Antonio, Gonzalo, Adrian, Francisco, *and others.*]

Gonzalo [*to* Alonso]. Beseech you, sir, be merry. You
  have cause—
So have we all—of joy, for our escape
Is much beyond our loss. Our hint of woe
Is common; every day some sailor's wife,
5 The masters of some merchant, and the merchant
Have just our theme of woe. But for the miracle—
I mean our preservation—few in millions
Can speak like us. Then wisely, good sir, weigh
Our sorrow with our comfort.

Alonso. Prithee, peace.

10 **Sebastian** [*aside to* Antonio]. He receives comfort like cold porridge.

Antonio. The visitor will not give him o'er so.

Sebastian. Look, he's winding up the watch of his wit. By and by it will strike.

15 **Gonzalo** [*to* Alonso]. Sir—

Sebastian. One. Tell.

Gonzalo. When every grief is entertained that's offered, comes to th' entertainer—

Sebastian. A dollar.

20 **Gonzalo.** Dolor comes to him indeed. You have spoken truer than you purposed.

The Tempest 49

26 *spare:* spare your words.

30–32 *first begins to crow:* will speak first. (Sebastian and Antonio allude to the proverbial saying "The young cock (*cockerel*) crows as he the old hears.")

34 *A laughter:* Antonio alludes to the saying "He laughs that wins."

36 *desert:* deserted.

44 *temperance:* climate (also a woman's name, which inspires Antonio's punning response).

Sebastian. You have taken it wiselier than I meant you should.

Gonzalo [*to* Alonso]. Therefore, my lord—

25 **Antonio.** Fie, what a spendthrift is he of his tongue.

Alonso [*to* Gonzalo]. I prithee, spare.

Gonzalo. Well, I have done. But yet—

Sebastian [*aside to* Antonio]. He will be talking.

Antonio [*aside to* Sebastian]. Which, of he or Adrian,
30   for a good wager, first begins to crow?

Sebastian. The old cock.

Antonio. The cockerel.

Sebastian. Done. The wager?

Antonio. A laughter.

35 **Sebastian.** A match!

Adrian. Though this island seem to be desert—

Antonio. Ha, ha, ha.

Sebastian. So. You're paid.

Adrian. Uninhabitable and almost inaccessible—

40 **Sebastian.** Yet—

Adrian. Yet—

Antonio. He could not miss 't.

Adrian. It must needs be of subtle, tender, and delicate temperance.

45 **Antonio.** Temperance was a delicate wench.

Sebastian. Ay, and a subtle, as he most learnedly delivered.

Adrian. The air breathes upon us here most sweetly.

The Tempest   51

52 *save:* except for.

54 *lush and lusty:* abundant and vigorous.

56 *tawny:* yellowish-brown (parched by the sun).
57 *eye:* tinge.

60 *rarity:* exceptional quality.

62 *vouched rarities:* alleged wonders.

69 *pocket up:* conceal; suppress.

71 *Afric:* Africa.

77 *to:* for.

Sebastian. As if it had lungs, and rotten ones.

Antonio. Or as 'twere perfumed by a fen.

Gonzalo. Here is everything advantageous to life.

Antonio. True, save means to live.

Sebastian. Of that there's none, or little.

Gonzalo. How lush and lusty the grass looks! How green!

Antonio. The ground indeed is tawny.

Sebastian. With an eye of green in 't.

Antonio. He misses not much.

Sebastian. No, he doth but mistake the truth totally.

Gonzalo. But the rarity of it is, which is indeed almost beyond credit—

Sebastian. As many vouched rarities are.

Gonzalo. That our garments, being, as they were, drenched in the sea, hold notwithstanding their freshness and gloss, being rather new-dyed than stained with salt water.

Antonio. If but one of his pockets could speak, would it not say he lies?

Sebastian. Ay, or very falsely pocket up his report.

Gonzalo. Methinks our garments are now as fresh as when we put them on first in Afric, at the marriage of the King's fair daughter Claribel to the King of Tunis.

Sebastian. 'Twas a sweet marriage, and we prosper well in our return.

Adrian. Tunis was never graced before with such a paragon to their queen.

78 **Dido:** a queen of Carthage who, in Virgil's *Aeneid*, commits suicide after Aeneas abandons her.

84 **study of:** think about.

86 Tunis was built near the site of Carthage.

89 **miraculous harp:** In Greek mythology, Amphion used his harp to raise a wall around Thebes. (Antonio suggests that Gonzalo has surpassed this feat by raising an entire city.)

95 **kernels:** seeds.

97 **Ay:** probably an affirmation of his earlier statement that Tunis was Carthage.

104 **Bate:** except for.

Gonzalo. Not since widow Dido's time.

Antonio. Widow? A pox o' that! How came that "widow" in? Widow Dido!

Sebastian. What if he had said "widower Aeneas" too? Good Lord, how you take it!

Adrian [*to* Gonzalo]. "Widow Dido," said you? You make me study of that. She was of Carthage, not of Tunis.

Gonzalo. This Tunis, sir, was Carthage.

Adrian. Carthage?

Gonzalo. I assure you, Carthage.

Antonio. His word is more than the miraculous harp.

Sebastian. He hath raised the wall, and houses too.

Antonio. What impossible matter will he make easy next?

Sebastian. I think he will carry this island home in his pocket and give it his son for an apple.

Antonio. And sowing the kernels of it in the sea, bring forth more islands.

Gonzalo. Ay.

Antonio. Why, in good time.

Gonzalo [*to* Alonso]. Sir, we were talking that our garments seem now as fresh as when we were at Tunis at the marriage of your daughter, who is now queen.

Antonio. And the rarest that e'er came there.

Sebastian. Bate, I beseech you, widow Dido.

Antonio. O, widow Dido? Ay, widow Dido.

107 *in a sort:* to some extent.

108 *sort:* lot (in the game of drawing lots).

111–112 *against . . . sense:* although I am in no mood to hear them.

114 *rate:* estimation.

119 *surges:* waves.

124 *lusty:* vigorous.

125–126 *that o'er . . . him:* The cliff at the shoreline, eroded at its base by waves, seemed as if it were stooping over to help Ferdinand.

132 *Who . . . on't:* you who have reason to weep over the sorrow of it.

133 *importuned otherwise:* begged to change your decision.

134–136 *the fair . . . bow:* Claribel weighed her distaste for the marriage against her wish to obey Alonso, to see which end of the scale would sink.

Gonzalo [*to* Alonso]. Is not, sir, my doublet as fresh as
the first day I wore it? I mean, in a sort.

Antonio. That "sort" was well fished for.

Gonzalo [*to* Alonso]. When I wore it at your daughter's
marriage.

Alonso. You cram these words into mine ears against
The stomach of my sense. Would I had never
Married my daughter there, for coming thence
My son is lost, and, in my rate, she too,
Who is so far from Italy removed
I ne'er again shall see her.—O, thou mine heir
Of Naples and of Milan, what strange fish
Hath made his meal on thee?

Francisco.   Sir, he may live.
I saw him beat the surges under him
And ride upon their backs. He trod the water,
Whose enmity he flung aside, and breasted
The surge most swoll'n that met him. His bold head
'Bove the contentious waves he kept, and oared
Himself with his good arms in lusty stroke
To th' shore, that o'er his wave-worn basis bowed,
As stooping to relieve him. I not doubt
He came alive to land.

Alonso.   No, no, he's gone.

Sebastian. Sir, you may thank yourself for this great loss,
That would not bless our Europe with your daughter,
But rather lose her to an African,
Where she at least is banished from your eye,
Who hath cause to wet the grief on 't.

Alonso.   Prithee, peace.

Sebastian. You were kneeled to and importuned
otherwise
By all of us; and the fair soul herself
Weighed between loathness and obedience at

140 dear'st: most costly.

143 time: the appropriate time.
144 plaster: a medicinal paste applied to the body.

145 chirurgeonly: like a surgeon.

148 Had I plantation: if I were responsible for colonizing. (Antonio's response plays with the meaning "planting.")
149 nettle seed . . . docks . . . mallows: types of weeds.

152–153 by contraries . . . things: carry out everything in a manner opposite to what is customary.
153 traffic: commerce.

155 Letters: writing learning.
156 use of service: employment of servants; **succession:** inheritance.
157 Bourn: boundary; **tilth:** cultivation of land.
158 corn: grain.

>   Which end o' th' beam should bow. We have lost your son,
>   I fear, forever. Milan and Naples have
>   More widows in them of this business' making
>   Than we bring men to comfort them.
> 140 The fault's your own.
>
> **Alonso.** So is the dear'st o' th' loss.
>
> **Gonzalo.** My lord Sebastian,
>   The truth you speak doth lack some gentleness
>   And time to speak it in. You rub the sore
>   When you should bring the plaster.
>
> **Sebastian.** Very well.
>
> 145 **Antonio.** And most chirurgeonly.
>
> **Gonzalo** [*to* Alonso]. It is foul weather in us all, good sir,
>   When you are cloudy.
>
> **Sebastian.** Foul weather?
>
> **Antonio.** Very foul.
>
> **Gonzalo.** Had I plantation of this isle, my lord—
>
> **Antonio.** He'd sow 't with nettle seed.
>
> **Sebastian.** Or docks, or mallows.
>
> 150 **Gonzalo.** And were the King on 't, what would I do?
>
> **Sebastian.** Scape being drunk, for want of wine.
>
> **Gonzalo.** I' th' commonwealth I would by contraries
>   Execute all things, for no kind of traffic
>   Would I admit; no name of magistrate;
> 155 Letters should not be known; riches, poverty,
>   And use of service, none; contract, succession,
>   Bourn, bound of land, tilth, vineyard, none;
>   No use of metal, corn, or wine, or oil;
>   No occupation; all men idle, all,
> 160 And women too, but innocent and pure;
>   No sovereignty—

164 *in common:* for communal use.

166 *engine:* weapon.

168 *foison:* plenty.

173 *'Save:* God save.

177 *minister occasion:* provide an opportunity.
178 *sensible:* sensitive; ***use:*** are accustomed.

185 *An it . . . flatlong:* if it had not been given with the flat of the sword (rather than the edge).
186 *mettle:* temperament.
187 *sphere:* orbit.

Sebastian. Yet he would be king on 't.

Antonio. The latter end of his commonwealth forgets the beginning.

Gonzalo. All things in common nature should produce
165 Without sweat or endeavor; treason, felony,
Sword, pike, knife, gun, or need of any engine
Would I not have; but nature should bring forth
Of its own kind all foison, all abundance,
To feed my innocent people.

170 **Sebastian.** No marrying 'mong his subjects?

Antonio. None, man, all idle: whores and knaves.

Gonzalo. I would with such perfection govern, sir, T' excel the Golden Age.

Sebastian. 'Save his Majesty!

Antonio. Long live Gonzalo!

Gonzalo. And do you mark me, sir?

175 **Alonso.** Prithee, no more. Thou dost talk nothing to me.

Gonzalo. I do well believe your Highness, and did it to minister occasion to these gentlemen, who are of such sensible and nimble lungs that they always use to laugh at nothing.

180 **Antonio.** 'Twas you we laughed at.

Gonzalo. Who in this kind of merry fooling am nothing to you. So you may continue, and laugh at nothing still.

Antonio. What a blow was there given!

185 **Sebastian.** An it had not fallen flatlong.

Gonzalo. You are gentlemen of brave mettle. You would lift the moon out of her sphere if she would continue in it five weeks without changing.

189 *a-batfowling:* hunting birds at night with a stick. (Sebastian proposes using the moon for a lantern).

191–192 *adventure . . . weakly:* risk my reputation by behaving so weakly.
193 *heavy:* sleepy.

198 *omit:* neglect.

208 *consent:* agreement.

62   Literature Connections

[*Enter* Ariel, *invisible, playing solemn music.*]

Sebastian. We would so, and then go a-batfowling.

190 **Antonio** [*to* Gonzalo]. Nay, good my lord, be not angry.

Gonzalo. No, I warrant you, I will not adventure my discretion so weakly. Will you laugh me asleep? For I am very heavy.

Antonio. Go sleep, and hear us.

[*All sink down asleep except* Alonso, Antonio, *and* Sebastian.]

195 **Alonso.** What, all so soon asleep? I wish mine eyes
Would, with themselves, shut up my thoughts. I find
They are inclined to do so.

Sebastian. Please you, sir,
Do not omit the heavy offer of it.
It seldom visits sorrow; when it doth,
200 It is a comforter.

Antonio. We two, my lord,
Will guard your person while you take your rest,
And watch your safety.

Alonso. Thank you. Wondrous heavy.

[Alonso *sleeps.* Ariel *exits.*]

Sebastian. What a strange drowsiness possesses them!

Antonio. It is the quality o' th' climate.

Sebastian. Why
205 Doth it not then our eyelids sink? I find
Not myself disposed to sleep.

Antonio. Nor I. My spirits are nimble.
They fell together all, as by consent.
They dropped as by a thunderstroke. What might,
210 Worthy Sebastian, O, what might—? No more.
And yet methinks I see it in thy face

212 Th' occasion speaks thee: the opportunity calls out to you.

214 waking: awake.

221 wink'st: you close your eyes.

222 distinctly: in a way that can be understood.

225 if heed me: if you pay attention to me.
226 Trebles thee o'er: makes you three times as great; **standing water:** stagnant water (waiting to hear what Antonio has to say).

227–228 To ebb . . . me: I already know how to recede from my natural laziness (or status as a younger brother).

229 the purpose cherish: foster the intention (of becoming king).
231 invest it: clothe it; **Ebbing:** unsuccessful.

234 setting: fixed expression.
235 A matter: something important.
236 throes thee much to yield: causes you great pain to give forth (as in childbirth).

What thou shouldst be. Th' occasion speaks thee, and
My strong imagination sees a crown
Dropping upon thy head.

Sebastian. What, art thou waking?

Antonio. Do you not hear me speak?

Sebastian. I do, and surely
It is a sleepy language, and thou speak'st
Out of thy sleep. What is it thou didst say?
This is a strange repose, to be asleep
With eyes wide open—standing, speaking, moving—
And yet so fast asleep.

Antonio. Noble Sebastian,
Thou let'st thy fortune sleep, die rather, wink'st
Whiles thou art waking.

Sebastian. Thou dost snore distinctly.
There's meaning in thy snores.

Antonio. I am more serious than my custom. You
Must be so too, if heed me; which to do
Trebles thee o'er.

Sebastian. Well, I am standing water.

Antonio. I'll teach you how to flow.

Sebastian. Do so. To ebb
Hereditary sloth instructs me.

Antonio. O,
If you but knew how you the purpose cherish
Whiles thus you mock it, how in stripping it
You more invest it. Ebbing men indeed
Most often do so near the bottom run
By their own fear or sloth.

Sebastian. Prithee, say on.
The setting of thine eye and cheek proclaim
A matter from thee, and a birth indeed
Which throes thee much to yield.

237 **remembrance:** memory.
238 **of as little memory:** as quickly forgotten.
239 **earthed:** buried.
240–241 **only . . . persuade:** his only profession is to persuade.

245 **that way:** of Ferdinand's being alive.

247–248 **cannot pierce . . . there:** cannot set its sight on any higher goal.

252 **beyond man's life:** farther than one could travel in a lifetime.
253 **note:** information; **post:** the messenger.
254–255 **till new-born . . . razorable:** until enough time passed for a baby boy to become old enough to shave.
255 **from:** coming from.
256 **cast again:** cast ashore or cast into new roles.

259 **discharge:** performance.

Antonio. Thus, sir:
Although this lord of weak remembrance—this,
Who shall be of as little memory
When he is earthed—hath here almost persuaded—
240 For he's a spirit of persuasion, only
Professes to persuade—the King his son's alive,
'Tis as impossible that he's undrowned
As he that sleeps here swims.

Sebastian. I have no hope
That he's undrowned.

Antonio. O, out of that no hope
245 What great hope have you! No hope that way is
Another way so high a hope that even
Ambition cannot pierce a wink beyond,
But doubt discovery there. Will you grant with me
That Ferdinand is drowned?

Sebastian. He's gone.

Antonio. Then tell me,
250 Who's the next heir of Naples?

Sebastian. Claribel.

Antonio. She that is Queen of Tunis; she that dwells
Ten leagues beyond man's life; she that from Naples
Can have no note, unless the sun were post—
The man i' th' moon's too slow—till newborn chins
255 Be rough and razorable; she that from whom
We all were sea-swallowed, though some cast again,
And by that destiny to perform an act
Whereof what's past is prologue, what to come
In yours and my discharge.

260 **Sebastian.** What stuff is this? How say you?
'Tis true my brother's daughter's Queen of Tunis,
So is she heir of Naples, 'twixt which regions
There is some space.

263 ***cubit:*** an ancient unit of measure varying from 17 to 22 inches.

265 ***Measure us:*** travel over our length; ***Keep:*** stay.

266–267 ***Say this . . . them:*** suppose that death rather than sleep had overtaken Alonso and Gonzalo. *What do you think Antonio is hinting at?*

268 ***that:*** those who.

269 ***prate:*** babble.

271–272 ***make . . . chat:*** train a jackdaw (a bird related to the crow) to speak as profoundly.

275–276 ***how does . . . Tender:*** what do you think of.

279 ***feater:*** more suitably.

282–283 ***If 'twere . . . slipper:*** if it were a sore on my heel, it would force me to wear slippers.

285 ***candied:*** covered with frost; frozen.

289 ***steel:*** sword.

291 ***To the . . . put:*** might put to sleep forever.

294 ***take suggestion:*** accept temptation.

Antonio. A space whose ev'ry cubit
Seems to cry out "How shall that Claribel
Measure us back to Naples? Keep in Tunis
And let Sebastian wake." Say this were death
That now hath seized them, why, they were no worse
Than now they are. There be that can rule Naples
As well as he that sleeps, lords that can prate
As amply and unnecessarily
As this Gonzalo. I myself could make
A chough of as deep chat. O, that you bore
The mind that I do, what a sleep were this
For your advancement! Do you understand me?

Sebastian. Methinks I do.

Antonio. And how does your content
Tender your own good fortune?

Sebastian. I remember
You did supplant your brother Prospero.

Antonio. True,
And look how well my garments sit upon me,
Much feater than before. My brother's servants
Were then my fellows; now they are my men.

Sebastian. But, for your conscience?

Antonio. Ay, sir, where lies that? If 'twere a kibe,
'Twould put me to my slipper, but I feel not
This deity in my bosom. Twenty consciences
That stand 'twixt me and Milan, candied be they
And melt ere they molest! Here lies your brother,
No better than the earth he lies upon.
If he were that which now he's like—that's dead—
Whom I with this obedient steel, three inches of it,
Can lay to bed forever; whiles you, doing thus,
To the perpetual wink for aye might put
This ancient morsel, this Sir Prudence, who
Should not upbraid our course. For all the rest,
They'll take suggestion as a cat laps milk.

The Tempest

295–296 tell the ... hour: agree to anything that we say is appropriate.

305 else: otherwise; **them:** Gonzalo and Alonso.

308 His time: its opportunity.

314 Why are you drawn?: Why have you drawn your weapons?
315 Wherefore: why; **ghastly:** fearful.

295 They'll tell the clock to any business that
We say befits the hour.

Sebastian. Thy case, dear friend,
Shall be my precedent: as thou got'st Milan,
I'll come by Naples. Draw thy sword. One stroke
Shall free thee from the tribute which thou payest,
300 And I the King shall love thee.

Antonio. Draw together,
And when I rear my hand, do you the like
To fall it on Gonzalo.

[*They draw their swords.*]

Sebastian. O, but one word.

[*They talk apart.*]

[*Enter* Ariel, *invisible, with music and song.*]

Ariel [*to the sleeping* Gonzalo]. My master through his art foresees the danger
That you, his friend, are in, and sends me forth—
305 For else his project dies—to keep them living.

[*sings in* Gonzalo's *ear:*]

> *While you here do snoring lie,*
> *Open-eyed conspiracy*
> *His time doth take.*
> *If of life you keep a care,*
310 *Shake off slumber and beware.*
> *Awake, awake!*

Antonio [*to* Sebastian]. Then let us both be sudden.

Gonzalo [*waking*]. Now, good angels preserve the King!

[*He wakes* Alonso.]

Alonso [*to* Sebastian]. Why, how now, ho! Awake? Why are you drawn?
315 Wherefore this ghastly looking?

316 *securing your repose:* guarding you while you slept.

326 *cried:* cried out.

328 *verily:* indeed true.

2 *flats:* swamps.

Gonzalo [*to* Sebastian]. What's the matter?

Sebastian. Whiles we stood here securing your repose,
Even now, we heard a hollow burst of bellowing
Like bulls, or rather lions. Did 't not wake you?
It struck mine ear most terribly.

Alonso. I heard nothing.

320 **Antonio.** O, 'twas a din to fright a monster's ear,
To make an earthquake. Sure, it was the roar
Of a whole herd of lions.

Alonso. Heard you this, Gonzalo?

Gonzalo. Upon mine honor, sir, I heard a humming,
325 And that a strange one too, which did awake me.
I shaked you, sir, and cried. As mine eyes opened,
I saw their weapons drawn. There was a noise,
That's verily. 'Tis best we stand upon our guard,
Or that we quit this place. Let's draw our weapons.

330 **Alonso.** Lead off this ground, and let's make further search
For my poor son.

Gonzalo. Heavens keep him from these beasts,
For he is, sure, i' th' island.

Alonso. Lead away.

Ariel [*aside*]. Prospero my lord shall know what I have done.
So, king, go safely on to seek thy son.

[*They exit.*]

Scene 2

[*Enter* Caliban *with a burden of wood. A noise of thunder heard.*]

Caliban. All the infections that the sun sucks up
From bogs, fens, flats, on Prosper fall and make him

3 ***By inchmeal:*** inch by inch.

5 ***urchin-shows:*** the appearance of goblins.
6 ***firebrand:*** piece of burning wood.

9 ***mow:*** grimace.

13 ***wound:*** entwined.

17 ***Perchance:*** perhaps; ***mind:*** notice.

18 ***bear off:*** ward off.

21 ***bombard:*** large leather jug.

27 ***poor-John:*** dried fish.

29–30 ***had but . . . silver:*** If I only had this fish painted on a sign at a fair, every fool on holiday there would pay a silver coin to see this curiosity.
31 ***make a man:*** make a man's fortune.
32 ***doit:*** small coin.

34 ***dead Indian:*** Native Americans were popular exhibits in Elizabethan England.

By inchmeal a disease! His spirits hear me,
And yet I needs must curse. But they'll nor pinch,
Fright me with urchin-shows, pitch me i' th' mire,
Nor lead me like a firebrand in the dark
Out of my way, unless he bid 'em. But
For every trifle are they set upon me,
Sometimes like apes, that mow and chatter at me
And after bite me; then like hedgehogs, which
Lie tumbling in my barefoot way and mount
Their pricks at my footfall. Sometime am I
All wound with adders, who with cloven tongues
Do hiss me into madness. Lo, now, lo!
Here comes a spirit of his, and to torment me
For bringing wood in slowly. I'll fall flat.
Perchance he will not mind me.

[*He lies down and covers himself with a cloak.*]

[*Enter* Trinculo.]

Trinculo. Here's neither bush nor shrub to bear off any weather at all. And another storm brewing; I hear it sing i' th' wind. Yond same black cloud, yond huge one, looks like a foul bombard that would shed his liquor. If it should thunder as it did before, I know not where to hide my head. Yond same cloud cannot choose but fall by pailfuls. [*noticing* Caliban] What have we here, a man or a fish? Dead or alive? A fish, he smells like a fish—a very ancient and fish-like smell, a kind of not-of-the-newest poor-John. A strange fish. Were I in England now, as once I was, and had but this fish painted, not a holiday fool there but would give a piece of silver. There would this monster make a man. Any strange beast there makes a man. When they will not give a doit to relieve a lame beggar, they will lay out ten to see a dead Indian. Legged like a man, and his fins like arms! Warm, o' my troth! I do now let loose my opinion, hold it no longer: this is no fish, but an

The Tempest 75

37 *suffered:* been killed.

39 *gaberdine:* cloak.

41 *shroud:* take shelter.
42 *dregs:* last drops.

47 *swabber:* sailor who cleans the deck.

51 *tang:* sting.

53 *pitch:* a sticky substance used for waterproofing. (Like tar, it was associated with sailors.)

59–60 *put tricks . . . Ind:* play pranks on me with illusions of savages and men of India.

62 *four legs:* Normally, this saying refers to men who walk on two legs.
63 *give ground:* retreat.
64 *at':* at the.

islander that hath lately suffered by a thunderbolt. [*thunder*] Alas, the storm is come again. My best way is to creep under his gaberdine. There is no other shelter hereabout. Misery acquaints a man with strange bedfellows. I will here shroud till the dregs of the storm be past.

[*He crawls under Caliban's cloak.*]

[*Enter* Stephano *singing.*]

Stephano. *I shall no more to sea, to sea.*
      Here shall I die ashore—
This is a very scurvy tune to sing at a man's funeral. Well, here's my comfort.

[*drinks*]

[*sings*]

The master, the swabber, the boatswain, and I,
    The gunner and his mate,
Loved Mall, Meg, and Marian, and Margery,
    But none of us cared for Kate.
      For she had a tongue with a tang,
      Would cry to a sailor "Go hang!"
She loved not the savor of tar nor of pitch,
Yet a tailor might scratch her where'er she did itch.
    Then to sea, boys, and let her go hang!
This is a scurvy tune too. But here's my comfort.

[*drinks*]

Caliban. Do not torment me! O!

Stephano. What's the matter? Have we devils here? Do you put tricks upon 's with savages and men of Ind? Ha? I have not scaped drowning to be afeard now of your four legs, for it hath been said "As proper a man as ever went on four legs cannot make him give ground," and it shall be said so again while Stephano breathes at' nostrils.

67 ague: a fever that causes shivering.

69 if it . . . that: if only because he speaks my language; **recover:** cure.

72 neat's leather: cowhide (shoes).

75 after: in the manner of.

77 afore: before; **go near to:** do much to.
78–79 I will . . . him: no price could be too high for him.

80 hath him: gets him.

89 chaps: jaws.

92 delicate: exquisitely made.

Caliban. The spirit torments me. O!

Stephano. This is some monster of the isle with four legs, who hath got, as I take it, an ague. Where the devil should he learn our language? I will give him some relief, if it be but for that. If I can recover him and keep him tame and get to Naples with him, he's a present for any emperor that ever trod on neat's leather.

Caliban. Do not torment me, prithee. I'll bring my wood home faster.

Stephano. He's in his fit now, and does not talk after the wisest. He shall taste of my bottle. If he have never drunk wine afore, it will go near to remove his fit. If I can recover him and keep him tame, I will not take too much for him. He shall pay for him that hath him, and that soundly.

Caliban. Thou dost me yet but little hurt. Thou wilt anon; I know it by thy trembling. Now Prosper works upon thee.

Stephano. Come on your ways. Open your mouth. Here is that which will give language to you, cat. Open your mouth. This will shake your shaking, I can tell you, and that soundly. [Caliban *drinks.*] You cannot tell who's your friend. Open your chaps again.

Trinculo. I should know that voice. It should be—but he is drowned, and these are devils. O, defend me!

Stephano. Four legs and two voices—a most delicate monster! His forward voice now is to speak well of his friend. His backward voice is to utter foul speeches and to detract. If all the wine in my bottle will recover him, I will help his ague. Come. [Caliban *drinks.*] Amen! I will pour some in thy other mouth.

Trinculo. Stephano!

101 ***long spoon:*** an allusion to the saying "He must have a long spoon that will eat with the devil."

109 ***siege:*** excrement; ***mooncalf:*** monstrosity; ***vent:*** excrete.

118 ***not constant:*** unsettled.
119 ***an if:*** if.
120 ***brave:*** splendid; noble.

124 ***butt of sack:*** barrel of wine.

Stephano. Doth thy other mouth call me? Mercy, mercy, this is a devil, and no monster! I will leave him; I have no long spoon.

Trinculo. Stephano! If thou be'st Stephano, touch me and speak to me, for I am Trinculo—be not afeard—thy good friend Trinculo.

Stephano. If thou be'st Trinculo, come forth. I'll pull thee by the lesser legs. If any be Trinculo's legs, these are they. [*He pulls him out from under Caliban's cloak.*] Thou art very Trinculo indeed. How cam'st thou to be the siege of this mooncalf? Can he vent Trinculos?

Trinculo. I took him to be killed with a thunderstroke. But art thou not drowned, Stephano? I hope now thou art not drowned. Is the storm overblown? I hid me under the dead mooncalf's gaberdine for fear of the storm. And art thou living, Stephano? O Stephano, two Neapolitans scaped!

Stephano. Prithee, do not turn me about. My stomach is not constant.

Caliban [*aside*]. These be fine things, an if they be not sprites. That's a brave god and bears celestial liquor. I will kneel to him.

[*He crawls out from under the cloak.*]

Stephano [*to* Trinculo]. How didst thou scape? How cam'st thou hither? Swear by this bottle how thou cam'st hither—I escaped upon a butt of sack, which the sailors heaved o'erboard—by this bottle, which I made of the bark of a tree with mine own hands, since I was cast ashore.

Caliban. I'll swear upon that bottle to be thy true subject, for the liquor is not earthly.

Stephano [*to* Trinculo]. Here. Swear then how thou escapedst.

134 ***kiss the book:*** an allusion to the custom of kissing the Bible to confirm an oath.

143 ***when time was:*** once upon a time.

145 ***mistress:*** Miranda; ***bush:*** bundle of sticks carried by the legendary man in the moon.

147 ***anon:*** shortly.

148 ***this good light:*** the sun.

151 ***drawn:*** drunk; ***sooth:*** truth.

154 ***perfidious:*** treacherous.

Trinculo. Swum ashore, man, like a duck. I can swim like a duck, I'll be sworn.

Stephano. Here, kiss the book. [Trinculo *drinks.*] Though thou canst swim like a duck, thou art made like a goose.

Trinculo. O Stephano, hast any more of this?

Stephano. The whole butt, man. My cellar is in a rock by th' seaside, where my wine is hid.—How now, mooncalf, how does thine ague?

Caliban. Hast thou not dropped from heaven?

Stephano. Out o' th' moon, I do assure thee. I was the man i' th' moon when time was.

Caliban. I have seen thee in her, and I do adore thee. My mistress showed me thee, and thy dog, and thy bush.

Stephano. Come, swear to that. Kiss the book. I will furnish it anon with new contents. Swear.

[Caliban *drinks.*]

Trinculo. By this good light, this is a very shallow monster. I afeard of him? A very weak monster. The man i' th' moon? A most poor, credulous monster!—Well drawn, monster, in good sooth!

Caliban. I'll show thee every fertile inch o' th' island, and I will kiss thy foot. I prithee, be my god.

Trinculo. By this light, a most perfidious and drunken monster. When 's god's asleep, he'll rob his bottle.

Caliban. I'll kiss thy foot. I'll swear myself thy subject.

Stephano. Come on, then. Down, and swear.

[Caliban *kneels.*]

Trinculo. I shall laugh myself to death at this puppy-headed monster. A most scurvy monster. I could find in my heart to beat him—

162 *in drink:* drunk.

172 *pignuts:* edible tubers (similar to peanuts).

174 *marmoset:* a small monkey.

176 *scamels:* possibly a misspelling of *sea-mels,* meaning "gulls."

179–180 *inherit here:* take possession of this place.

184 *for:* to catch.
185 *firing:* firewood.

187 *trenchering:* wooden plates.

Stephano. Come, kiss.

Trinculo. But that the poor monster's in drink. An abominable monster.

Caliban. I'll show thee the best springs. I'll pluck thee berries.
165 I'll fish for thee and get thee wood enough.
A plague upon the tyrant that I serve.
I'll bear him no more sticks, but follow thee,
Thou wondrous man.

Trinculo. A most ridiculous monster, to make a wonder
170 of a poor drunkard.

Caliban [*standing*]. I prithee, let me bring thee where crabs grow,
And I with my long nails will dig thee pignuts,
Show thee a jay's nest, and instruct thee how
To snare the nimble marmoset. I'll bring thee
175 To clustering filberts, and sometimes I'll get thee
Young scamels from the rock. Wilt thou go with me?

Stephano. I prithee now, lead the way without any more talking.—Trinculo, the King and all our company else being drowned, we will inherit
180 here.—Here, bear my bottle.—Fellow Trinculo, we'll fill him by and by again.

Caliban [*sings drunkenly*].
    Farewell, master, farewell, farewell.

Trinculo. A howling monster, a drunken monster.

Caliban [*sings*].
    No more dams I'll make for fish,
185   Nor fetch in firing
        At requiring,
    Nor scrape trenchering, nor wash dish.
    'Ban, 'ban, Ca-caliban
    Has a new master. Get a new man.

190 *high-day:* holiday.

190 Freedom, high-day! High-day, freedom! Freedom, high-day, freedom!

Stephano. O brave monster! Lead the way.

[*They exit.*]

1–2 ***their labor . . . sets off:*** our enjoyment of them takes away their pains.
  2 ***baseness:*** menial work.
  3 ***undergone:*** undertaken.
  4 ***mean:*** lowly.
  5 ***but:*** except that.
  6 ***quickens:*** revives.

  11 ***sore injunction:*** harsh command.

  13 ***Had never like executor:*** never had such a person performing it.
13–15 ***I forget . . . do it:*** I'm neglecting my work, but my head is most filled with these sweet thoughts when I am working.

  17 ***enjoined:*** ordered.

  21 ***safe:*** unable to harm us.

ACT THREE

Scene 1

[*Enter* Ferdinand *bearing a log.*]

Ferdinand. There be some sports are painful, and
   their labor
Delight in them sets off; some kinds of baseness
Are nobly undergone; and most poor matters
Point to rich ends. This my mean task
5 Would be as heavy to me as odious, but
The mistress which I serve quickens what's dead
And makes my labors pleasures. O, she is
Ten times more gentle than her father's crabbed,
And he's composed of harshness. I must remove
10 Some thousands of these logs and pile them up,
Upon a sore injunction. My sweet mistress
Weeps when she sees me work, and says such
   baseness
Had never like executor. I forget,
But these sweet thoughts do even refresh my labors,
15 Most busiest when I do it.

[*Enter* Miranda; *and* Prospero *at a distance, unobserved.*]

Miranda.   Alas now, pray you,
Work not so hard. I would the lightning had
Burnt up those logs that you are enjoined to pile.
Pray, set it down and rest you. When this burns
'Twill weep for having wearied you. My father
20 Is hard at study. Pray now, rest yourself.
He's safe for these three hours.

Ferdinand.   O most dear mistress,
The sun will set before I shall discharge
What I must strive to do.

32 worm: creature; ***infected:*** lovesick.
33 visitation: visit.

38 hest: command; ***Admired:*** Miranda's name means "admirable" or "wonderful" in Latin.

43 diligent: attentive; ***several:*** different; various.

45 with so full soul: with my entire heart.
46 owed: owned.
47 put it to the foil: overthrew it (a fencing term).

49 best: best qualities.

Miranda. If you'll sit down,
I'll bear your logs the while. Pray, give me that.
I'll carry it to the pile.

Ferdinand. No, precious creature,
I had rather crack my sinews, break my back,
Than you should such dishonor undergo
While I sit lazy by.

Miranda. It would become me
As well as it does you, and I should do it
With much more ease, for my good will is to it,
And yours it is against.

Prospero [*aside*]. Poor worm, thou art infected.
This visitation shows it.

Miranda. You look wearily.

Ferdinand. No, noble mistress, 'tis fresh morning with me
When you are by at night. I do beseech you,
Chiefly that I might set it in my prayers,
What is your name?

Miranda. Miranda.—O my father,
I have broke your hest to say so!

Ferdinand. Admired Miranda!
Indeed the top of admiration, worth
What's dearest to the world! Full many a lady
I have eyed with best regard, and many a time
Th' harmony of their tongues hath into bondage
Brought my too diligent ear. For several virtues
Have I liked several women, never any
With so full soul but some defect in her
Did quarrel with the noblest grace she owed,
And put it to the foil. But you, O you,
So perfect and so peerless, are created
Of every creature's best.

Miranda. I do not know
One of my sex, no woman's face remember,

51 *glass:* mirror.

53–54 *How features . . . skilless of:* I have no knowledge of what people look like elsewhere.
54 *modesty:* virginity.
55 *jewel in my dower:* my most precious possession; *wish:* wish for.
57–58 *Nor can . . . like of:* nor can I imagine preferring anyone's appearance to yours.
59 *Something:* somewhat; *precepts:* orders.

61 *condition:* social position.

63 *I would, not so:* I wish it were not so.
64 *wooden slavery:* carrying logs.
65 *flesh-fly:* an insect that deposits eggs in dead flesh; *blow:* deposit eggs in.

71 *kind event:* favorable outcome.
72–73 *if hollowly . . . mischief:* If I speak falsely, turn the brightest moments of my future into misfortune.

78 *Wherefore:* why.

81 *want:* lack; *trifling:* frivolous talk.

92   **Literature Connections**

Save, from my glass, mine own. Nor have I seen
More that I may call men than you, good friend,
And my dear father. How features are abroad
I am skilless of, but by my modesty,
The jewel in my dower, I would not wish
Any companion in the world but you,
Nor can imagination form a shape
Besides yourself to like of. But I prattle
Something too wildly, and my father's precepts
I therein do forget.

Ferdinand. I am in my condition
A prince, Miranda; I do think a king—
I would, not so!—and would no more endure
This wooden slavery than to suffer
The flesh-fly blow my mouth. Hear my soul speak:
The very instant that I saw you did
My heart fly to your service, there resides
To make me slave to it, and for your sake
Am I this patient log-man.

Miranda.   Do you love me?

Ferdinand. O heaven, O earth, bear witness to this sound,
And crown what I profess with kind event
If I speak true; if hollowly, invert
What best is boded me to mischief. I,
Beyond all limit of what else i' th' world,
Do love, prize, honor you.

Miranda.   I am a fool
To weep at what I am glad of.

Prospero [*aside*].   Fair encounter
Of two most rare affections. Heavens rain grace
On that which breeds between 'em!

Ferdinand.   Wherefore weep you?

Miranda. At mine unworthiness, that dare not offer
What I desire to give, and much less take
What I shall die to want. But this is trifling,

83 *bashful cunning:* cunning shyness.

86 *maid:* virgin or servant; *fellow:* companion or equal.

89 *mistress:* sweetheart.

90–91 *as willing . . . freedom:* as eager for it as a slave is for freedom.

93 *thousand thousand:* million farewells.

95 *withal:* with it all.
96 *book:* book of magic.

98 *appertaining:* relating to this.

1–2 *butt is out:* barrel of wine is empty. *What sort of remark from Trinculo do you think Stephano is responding to?*

3 *bear up and board 'em:* drink up.

7 *be brained like us:* have brains like ours.

And all the more it seeks to hide itself,
The bigger bulk it shows. Hence, bashful cunning,
And prompt me, plain and holy innocence.
85   I am your wife if you will marry me.
If not, I'll die your maid. To be your fellow
You may deny me, but I'll be your servant
Whether you will or no.

Ferdinand. My mistress, dearest, and I thus humble ever.

90   **Miranda.** My husband, then?

Ferdinand.   Ay, with a heart as willing
As bondage e'er of freedom. Here's my hand.

Miranda [*clasping his hand*]. And mine, with my heart
  in 't. And now farewell
Till half an hour hence.

Ferdinand.   A thousand thousand.

[*They exit.*]

Prospero. So glad of this as they I cannot be,
95   Who are surprised withal; but my rejoicing
At nothing can be more. I'll to my book,
For yet ere suppertime must I perform
Much business appertaining.

[*He exits.*]

Scene 2

[*Enter* Caliban, Stephano, *and* Trinculo.]

Stephano [*to* Trinculo]. Tell not me. When the butt is
out, we will drink water; not a drop before.
Therefore bear up and board 'em.—Servant
monster, drink to me.

5   **Trinculo.** Servant monster? The folly of this island!
They say there's but five upon this isle; we are three
of them. If th' other two be brained like us, the state
totters.

10 *set in:* sunk into (from drunkenness).

11 *set:* placed.

15 *recover:* reach.
15–16 *five-and-thirty leagues:* about a hundred miles.

17 *standard:* standard-bearer.

18 *list:* wish; *he's no standard:* he can't stand up.

19 *run:* run from an enemy.

20 *go:* walk; *lie:* lie down or tell lies.

26–27 *in case to justle:* in a condition (because he's drunk) to jostle.

34 *natural:* idiot (monsters are often called unnatural).

37 *the next tree:* you will hang on the next tree.

Stephano. Drink, servant monster, when I bid thee. Thy eyes are almost set in thy head.

[Caliban *drinks.*]

Trinculo. Where should they be set else? He were a brave monster indeed if they were set in his tail.

Stephano. My man-monster hath drowned his tongue in sack. For my part, the sea cannot drown me. I swam, ere I could recover the shore, five-and-thirty leagues off and on, by this light.—Thou shalt be my lieutenant, monster, or my standard.

Trinculo. Your lieutenant, if you list. He's no standard.

Stephano. We'll not run, Monsieur Monster.

Trinculo. Nor go neither. But you'll lie like dogs, and yet say nothing neither.

Stephano. Mooncalf, speak once in thy life, if thou be'st a good mooncalf.

Caliban. How does thy Honor? Let me lick thy shoe. I'll not serve him; he is not valiant.

Trinculo. Thou liest, most ignorant monster. I am in case to justle a constable. Why, thou debauched fish, thou! Was there ever man a coward that hath drunk so much sack as I today? Wilt thou tell a monstrous lie, being but half a fish and half a monster?

Caliban. Lo, how he mocks me! Wilt thou let him, my lord?

Trinculo. "Lord," quoth he? That a monster should be such a natural!

Caliban. Lo, lo again! Bite him to death, I prithee.

Stephano. Trinculo, keep a good tongue in your head. If you prove a mutineer, the next tree. The poor monster's my subject, and he shall not suffer indignity.

41 ***suit:*** petition.

42 ***Marry:*** by the Virgin Mary (an exclamation similar to *indeed*).

47 What do you think Ariel intends to accomplish by imitating Trinculo's voice?

52 ***supplant:*** remove.

59 ***this thing:*** Trinculo.

62 ***compassed:*** achieved.

67 ***pied ninny:*** fool covered with patches of different colors (a jester's costume); ***patch:*** jester.

Caliban. I thank my noble lord. Wilt thou be pleased to harken once again to the suit I made to thee?

Stephano. Marry, will I. Kneel and repeat it. I will stand, and so shall Trinculo.

[*Enter* Ariel, *invisible.*]

Caliban [*kneeling*]. As I told thee before, I am subject to a tyrant, a sorcerer, that by his cunning hath cheated me of the island.

Ariel [*in Trinculo's voice*]. Thou liest.

Caliban [*to* Trinculo]. Thou liest, thou jesting monkey, thou. [*He stands.*] I would my valiant master would destroy thee. I do not lie.

Stephano. Trinculo, if you trouble him any more in 's tale, by this hand, I will supplant some of your teeth.

Trinculo. Why, I said nothing.

Stephano. Mum then, and no more. [Trinculo *stands aside.*] Proceed.

Caliban. I say by sorcery he got this isle;
From me he got it. If thy Greatness will,
Revenge it on him, for I know thou dar'st,
But this thing dare not.

Stephano. That's most certain.

Caliban. Thou shalt be lord of it, and I'll serve thee.

Stephano. How now shall this be compassed? Canst thou bring me to the party?

Caliban. Yea, yea, my lord. I'll yield him thee asleep, Where thou mayst knock a nail into his head.

Ariel [*in Trinculo's voice*]. Thou liest. Thou canst not.

Caliban. What a pied ninny's this!—Thou scurvy patch!—
I do beseech thy Greatness, give him blows

71 *quick freshes:* flowing streams.

75 *stockfish:* dried cod (which is beaten before being cooked).

81 *give me the lie:* call me a liar.

83–84 *This can . . . do:* This is what results from wine and drinking.
84 *murrain:* plague.

94 *There:* then.

96 *paunch him:* stab him in the belly.
97 *weasand:* throat.

99 *sot:* fool.

And take his bottle from him. When that's gone,
70 He shall drink naught but brine, for I'll not show him
Where the quick freshes are.

Stephano. Trinculo, run into no further danger.
Interrupt the monster one word further, and by this
hand, I'll turn my mercy out o' doors and make a
75 stockfish of thee.

Trinculo. Why, what did I? I did nothing. I'll go
farther off.

Stephano. Didst thou not say he lied?

Ariel [*in Trinculo's voice*]. Thou liest.

80 **Stephano.** Do I so? Take thou that. [*He beats* Trinculo.]
As you like this, give me the lie another time.

Trinculo. I did not give the lie! Out o' your wits and
hearing too? A pox o' your bottle! This can sack and
drinking do. A murrain on your monster, and the
85 devil take your fingers!

Caliban. Ha, ha, ha!

Stephano. Now forward with your tale. [*to* Trinculo]
Prithee, stand further off.

Caliban. Beat him enough. After a little time
90 I'll beat him too.

Stephano. Stand farther. [Trinculo *moves farther away.*]
Come, proceed.

Caliban. Why, as I told thee, 'tis a custom with him
I' th' afternoon to sleep. There thou mayst brain him,
95 Having first seized his books, or with a log
Batter his skull, or paunch him with a stake,
Or cut his weasand with thy knife. Remember
First to possess his books, for without them
He's but a sot, as I am, nor hath not
100 One spirit to command. They all do hate him
As rootedly as I. Burn but his books.

102 *utensils:* household goods.

106 *nonpareil:* person without equal.

109 *brave:* fine.
110 *become:* suit.

113 *save:* God save.

123 *jocund:* cheerful; ***troll the catch:*** sing the song.
124 *but whilere:* just a while ago.

126 *any reason:* anything within reason.

127 *cout:* perhaps a nonsense word.
128 *scout:* mock.

He has brave utensils—for so he calls them—
Which, when he has a house, he'll deck withal.
And that most deeply to consider is
The beauty of his daughter. He himself
Calls her a nonpareil. I never saw a woman
But only Sycorax my dam and she;
But she as far surpasseth Sycorax
As great'st does least.

Stephano. Is it so brave a lass?

Caliban. Ay, lord, she will become thy bed, I warrant,
And bring thee forth brave brood.

Stephano. Monster, I will kill this man. His daughter and I will be king and queen—save our Graces!—and Trinculo and thyself shall be viceroys.—Dost thou like the plot, Trinculo?

Trinculo. Excellent.

Stephano. Give me thy hand. I am sorry I beat thee. But while thou liv'st, keep a good tongue in thy head.

Caliban. Within this half hour will he be asleep.
Wilt thou destroy him then?

Stephano. Ay, on mine honor.

Ariel [*aside*]. This will I tell my master.

Caliban. Thou mak'st me merry. I am full of pleasure.
Let us be jocund. Will you troll the catch
You taught me but whilere?

Stephano. At thy request, monster, I will do reason, any reason.—Come on, Trinculo, let us sing.

[*sings*]

> Flout 'em and cout 'em
> And scout 'em and flout 'em!
> Thought is free.

Caliban. That's not the tune.

Stage direction—*tabor:* a small drum; ***pipe:*** a wind instrument that can be played with one hand.

136 *list:* please.

143 *airs:* melodies.

154 *by and by:* soon.

158 *lays it on:* plays well.

[Ariel *plays the tune on a tabor and pipe.*]

Stephano. What is this same?

Trinculo. This is the tune of our catch played by the picture of Nobody.

Stephano [*to the invisible musician*]. If thou be'st a man, show thyself in thy likeness. If thou be'st a devil, take 't as thou list.

Trinculo. O, forgive me my sins!

Stephano. He that dies pays all debts.—I defy thee!— Mercy upon us.

Caliban. Art thou afeard?

Stephano. No, monster, not I.

Caliban. Be not afeard. The isle is full of noises,
Sounds and sweet airs that give delight and hurt not.
Sometimes a thousand twangling instruments
Will hum about mine ears, and sometimes voices
That, if I then had waked after long sleep,
Will make me sleep again; and then, in dreaming,
The clouds methought would open, and show riches
Ready to drop upon me, that when I waked
I cried to dream again.

Stephano. This will prove a brave kingdom to me, where I shall have my music for nothing.

Caliban. When Prospero is destroyed.

Stephano. That shall be by and by. I remember the story.

Trinculo. The sound is going away. Let's follow it, and after do our work.

Stephano. Lead, monster. We'll follow.—I would I could see this taborer. He lays it on. Wilt come?

Trinculo. I'll follow, Stephano.

[*They exit.*]

1 ***By 'r lakin:*** by our Lady (a mild oath).

3 ***forthrights and meanders:*** straight and winding paths.

5 ***attached:*** seized.

7 ***Even:*** exactly.

10 ***frustrate:*** vain.

12 ***for one repulse:*** because of one setback.

13 ***advantage:*** opportunity.
14 ***throughly:*** thoroughly.

Stage direction—*top:* a small platform above the stage.

20 ***keepers:*** guardian angels.

Scene 3

[*Enter* Alonso, Sebastian, Antonio, Gonzalo, Adrian, Francisco, *etc.*]

Gonzalo. By 'r lakin, I can go no further, sir.
My old bones aches. Here's a maze trod indeed
Through forthrights and meanders. By your patience,
I needs must rest me.

Alonso. Old lord, I cannot blame thee,
5 Who am myself attached with weariness
To th' dulling of my spirits. Sit down and rest.
Even here I will put off my hope and keep it
No longer for my flatterer. He is drowned
Whom thus we stray to find, and the sea mocks
10 Our frustrate search on land. Well, let him go.

Antonio [*aside to* Sebastian]. I am right glad that he's so
out of hope.
Do not, for one repulse, forgo the purpose
That you resolved t' effect.

Sebastian [*aside to* Antonio]. The next advantage
Will we take throughly.

Antonio [*aside to* Sebastian]. Let it be tonight;
15 For now they are oppressed with travel, they
Will not nor cannot use such vigilance
As when they are fresh.

Sebastian [*aside to* Antonio]. I say tonight. No more.

[*Solemn and strange music, and enter* Prospero *on the top invisible.*]

Alonso. What harmony is this? My good friends, hark.

Gonzalo. Marvelous sweet music!

[*Enter several strange shapes, bringing in a banquet, and dance about it with gentle actions of salutations.*]

20 **Alonso.** Give us kind keepers, heavens! What were these?

21 ***drollery:*** puppet show or comic picture.

23 ***phoenix:*** a mythical bird of which only one exists at a time, nesting in a single tree in Arabia.

25 ***what does else want credit:*** whatever else is incredible.
26 ***Travelers:*** Travelers had a reputation for being liars.

30 ***certes:*** certainly.

36 ***muse:*** marvel at.

39 ***dumb discourse:*** silent speech; ***Praise in departing:*** Hold your praise until the end.

42 ***viands:*** dishes of food; ***stomachs:*** appetites.

Sebastian. A living drollery! Now I will believe
That there are unicorns, that in Arabia
There is one tree, the phoenix' throne, one phoenix
At this hour reigning there.

Antonio.   I'll believe both;
25   And what does else want credit, come to me
And I'll be sworn 'tis true. Travelers ne'er did lie,
Though fools at home condemn 'em.

Gonzalo.   If in Naples
I should report this now, would they believe me?
If I should say I saw such islanders—
30   For, certes, these are people of the island—
Who, though they are of monstrous shape, yet note
Their manners are more gentle, kind, than of
Our human generation you shall find
Many, nay, almost any.

Prospero [*aside*].   Honest lord,
35   Thou hast said well, for some of you there present
Are worse than devils.

Alonso.   I cannot too much muse
Such shapes, such gesture, and such sound, expressing—
Although they want the use of tongue—a kind
Of excellent dumb discourse.

Prospero [*aside*].   Praise in departing.

[*Inviting the King, etc., to eat, the shapes depart.*]

40   **Francisco.** They vanished strangely.

Sebastian. No matter, since
They have left their viands behind, for we have stomachs.
Will 't please you taste of what is here?

Alonso.   Not I.

Gonzalo. Faith, sir, you need not fear. When we were boys,

45 ***mountaineers:*** mountain dwellers.
46 ***Dewlapped:*** with folds of skin under their throats.
47 ***Wallets:*** wattles.

49–50 ***Each putter-out . . . warrant of:*** each traveler will guarantee to be true. (Elizabethan travelers could leave a deposit with a London broker and be repaid fivefold if they provided proof that they had reached their destination. Travelers often returned with fantastic tales such as the ones Gonzalo refers to in this speech.)
50 ***stand to and feed:*** begin eating.

Stage direction—*Harpy:* a mythological monster that is part woman and part bird; ***quaint device:*** ingenious mechanism.

54–57 ***Destiny . . . up you:*** Destiny, which uses the entire world as its instrument, has caused the insatiable sea to belch you up.

60 ***such-like valor:*** the courage of madmen.
61 ***Their proper selves:*** themselves.

63 ***tempered:*** compounded.
64 ***bemocked-at:*** ridiculed.
65 ***still-closing:*** always closing up after being parted.
66 ***dowl:*** tiny feather; ***plume:*** plumage; ***ministers:*** agents.
67 ***like:*** similarly.
68 ***massy:*** heavy.

45 Who would believe that there were mountaineers
Dewlapped like bulls, whose throats had hanging
   at 'em
Wallets of flesh? Or that there were such men
Whose heads stood in their breasts? Which now
   we find
Each putter-out of five for one will bring us
50 Good warrant of.

Alonso.   I will stand to and feed.
Although my last, no matter, since I feel
The best is past. Brother, my lord the Duke,
Stand to, and do as we.

[Alonso, Sebastian, *and* Antonio *move toward the table.*]

[*Thunder and lightning. Enter* Ariel, *like a Harpy, claps his wings upon the table, and with a quaint device the banquet vanishes.*]

Ariel [*as Harpy*]. You are three men of sin, whom Destiny,
55 That hath to instrument this lower world
And what is in 't, the never-surfeited sea
Hath caused to belch up you, and on this island,
Where man doth not inhabit, you 'mongst men
Being most unfit to live. I have made you mad;
60 And even with such-like valor, men hang and drown
Their proper selves.

[Alonso, Sebastian, *and* Antonio *draw their swords.*]

                    You fools, I and my fellows
Are ministers of Fate. The elements
Of whom your swords are tempered may as well
Wound the loud winds or with bemocked-at stabs
65 Kill the still-closing waters as diminish
One dowl that's in my plume. My fellow ministers
Are like invulnerable. If you could hurt,
Your swords are now too massy for your strengths
And will not be uplifted. But remember—
70 For that's my business to you—that you three

The Tempest 111

72 **requit it:** avenged the deed.

78–80 **Ling'ring . . . ways:** slow destruction—worse than any quick death—will continually follow you.

80–83 **whose wraths . . . ensuing:** The only thing that can guard you from the wrath of the powers, which would otherwise strike you on this island, is repentance and leading a blameless life from now on.

Stage direction—*mocks and mows:* mockery and grimaces.

85 ***A grace it had, devouring:*** Your performance had a ravishing grace.

86 ***bated:*** omitted.

87–89 ***So, with . . . done:*** Likewise, my lesser spirits have carried out their various roles with vitality and remarkable attentiveness.

90 ***knit up:*** bound up; engrossed.

91 ***distractions:*** derangement.

From Milan did supplant good Prospero,
Exposed unto the sea, which hath requit it,
Him and his innocent child, for which foul deed,
The powers—delaying, not forgetting—have
Incensed the seas and shores, yea, all the creatures
Against your peace. Thee of thy son, Alonso,
They have bereft; and do pronounce by me
Ling'ring perdition, worse than any death
Can be at once, shall step by step attend
You and your ways, whose wraths to guard you from—
Which here, in this most desolate isle, else falls
Upon your heads—is nothing but heart's sorrow
And a clear life ensuing.

[*He vanishes in thunder.*]

[*Then, to soft music, enter the shapes again, and dance, with mocks and mows, and carrying out the table.*]

Prospero [*aside*]. Bravely the figure of this Harpy hast thou
Performed, my Ariel. A grace it had, devouring.
Of my instruction hast thou nothing bated
In what thou hadst to say. So, with good life
And observation strange, my meaner ministers
Their several kinds have done. My high charms work,
And these mine enemies are all knit up
In their distractions. They now are in my power;
And in these fits I leave them while I visit
Young Ferdinand, whom they suppose is drowned,
And his and mine loved darling.

[*He exits, above.*]

Gonzalo [*to Alonso*]. I' th' name of something holy, sir, why stand you
In this strange stare?

Alonso.   O, it is monstrous, monstrous!
Methought the billows spoke and told me of it;
The winds did sing it to me, and the thunder,

The Tempest   113

100 ***bass my trespass:*** sing my crime in a deep voice.
101 ***Therefor:*** for that.
102 ***plummet:*** a weight attached to a line; ***sounded:*** measured depth. *What action is Alonso planning to take?*

105 ***o'er:*** from beginning to end.

107 ***work:*** take effect.

110 ***ecstasy:*** madness.

That deep and dreadful organ pipe, pronounced
100 The name of Prosper. It did bass my trespass.
Therefor my son i' th' ooze is bedded, and
I'll seek him deeper than e'er plummet sounded,
And with him there lie mudded.

[*He exits.*]

Sebastian. But one fiend at a time,
105 I'll fight their legions o'er.

Antonio. I'll be thy second.

[*They exit.*]

Gonzalo. All three of them are desperate. Their great guilt,
Like poison given to work a great time after,
Now 'gins to bite the spirits. I do beseech you
That are of suppler joints, follow them swiftly
110 And hinder them from what this ecstasy
May now provoke them to.

Adrian. Follow, I pray you.

[*They all exit.*]

1 *austerely:* severely.

4 *who:* whom.
5 *tender:* offer.

7 *strangely:* wonderfully.

11 *halt:* limp.

12 *Against an oracle:* even if a message from a god declared otherwise.

14 *purchased:* earned.
15 *virgin-knot:* virginity.
16 *sanctimonious:* sacred.

18 *aspersion:* shower of grace.

23 *Hymen's lamps:* wedding torches; *light you:* show you the way. (In Greek mythology, Hymen is the god of marriage.)

24 *issue:* offspring.

ACT FOUR

Scene 1

[*Enter* Prospero, Ferdinand, *and* Miranda.]

Prospero [*to* Ferdinand]. If I have too austerely
    punished you,
    Your compensation makes amends, for I
    Have given you here a third of mine own life,
    Or that for which I live; who once again
5   I tender to thy hand. All thy vexations
    Were but my trials of thy love, and thou
    Hast strangely stood the test. Here afore heaven
    I ratify this my rich gift. O Ferdinand,
    Do not smile at me that I boast of her,
10   For thou shalt find she will outstrip all praise
    And make it halt behind her.

Ferdinand.   I do believe it
    Against an oracle.

Prospero. Then, as my gift and thine own acquisition
    Worthily purchased, take my daughter. But
15   If thou dost break her virgin-knot before
    All sanctimonious ceremonies may
    With full and holy rite be ministered,
    No sweet aspersion shall the heavens let fall
    To make this contract grow; but barren hate,
20   Sour-eyed disdain, and discord shall bestrew
    The union of your bed with weeds so loathly
    That you shall hate it both. Therefore take heed,
    As Hymen's lamps shall light you.

Ferdinand.   As I hope
    For quiet days, fair issue, and long life,

The Tempest

26 ***suggestion:*** temptation.
27 ***worser genius:*** bad angel; ***can:*** is capable of.

29 ***edge:*** keen desire.
30 ***or Phoebus' steeds are foundered:*** either the horses that pull the chariot of Phoebus, the sun god, have stumbled and gone lame. (Ferdinand's chastity will make him so impatient on his wedding day that it will seem as if night has been delayed.)

33 ***What:*** now then.

35 ***meaner fellows:*** lesser spirits.

37 ***rabble:*** mob of spirits.

41 ***vanity of mine art:*** trifling display of my magical powers.

42 ***Presently:*** immediately.
43 ***with a twink:*** in the twinkling of an eye.

47 ***mop and mow:*** grimaces.

50 ***conceive:*** understand.

25 With such love as 'tis now, the murkiest den,
    The most opportune place, the strong'st suggestion
    Our worser genius can shall never melt
    Mine honor into lust to take away
    The edge of that day's celebration
30 When I shall think or Phoebus' steeds are foundered
    Or night kept chained below.

Prospero.   Fairly spoke.
Sit then and talk with her. She is thine own.

[*Ferdinand and* Miranda *move aside.*]

What, Ariel, my industrious servant, Ariel!

[*Enter* Ariel.]

Ariel. What would my potent master? Here I am.

35 **Prospero.** Thou and thy meaner fellows your last service
    Did worthily perform, and I must use you
    In such another trick. Go bring the rabble,
    O'er whom I give thee power, here to this place.
    Incite them to quick motion, for I must
40 Bestow upon the eyes of this young couple
    Some vanity of mine art. It is my promise,
    And they expect it from me.

Ariel.   Presently?

Prospero. Ay, with a twink.

Ariel. Before you can say "Come" and "Go,"
45 And breathe twice, and cry "So, so,"
    Each one, tripping on his toe,
    Will be here with mop and mow.
    Do you love me, master? No?

Prospero. Dearly, my delicate Ariel. Do not approach
50 Till thou dost hear me call.

Ariel.   Well; I conceive.

[*He exits.*]

The Tempest

51 *true:* true to your word.
 51–52 *dalliance . . . rein:* too much free rein to flirtation.

 55–56 *The white . . . liver:* My chaste love for her diminishes my sexual passion.

 57 *corollary:* surplus.
 58 *want:* lack; *pertly:* briskly.

Stage direction—*Iris:* In Greek mythology, the goddess of the rainbow and messenger of the gods.
 60 *Ceres:* the Roman goddess of agriculture; *leas:* tracts of land.
 61 *vetches:* plants of a kind grown to feed livestock.
 63 *meads:* meadows; *stover:* a plant whose dried stalks and leaves are used for animal feed; *them to keep:* to feed the sheep.
 64 *pionèd and twillèd brims:* edges of riverbanks, covered with flowers or entwined branches.
 65 *Which . . . betrims:* which damp April adorns at your command.
 66 *cold:* chaste; *broom groves:* groups of shrubs.
 67 *dismissèd bachelor:* rejected suitor.
 68 *lass-lorn:* deprived of a girl; *poll-clipped:* pruned.
 69 *sea marge:* seashore.
 70 *air:* take the air; *Queen o' th' sky:* Juno (Jupiter's wife), the Roman queen of heaven and goddess of marriage.
 71 *wat'ry arch:* rainbow.

 74 *peacocks:* Juno's favorite birds; *amain:* in haste.

Prospero [*to* Ferdinand]. Look thou be true; do not give
    dalliance
Too much the rein. The strongest oaths are straw
To th' fire i' th' blood. Be more abstemious,
Or else goodnight your vow.

Ferdinand.   I warrant you, sir,
55   The white cold virgin snow upon my heart
Abates the ardor of my liver.

Prospero.   Well.—
Now come, my Ariel. Bring a corollary
Rather than want a spirit. Appear, and pertly.

[*soft music*]

No tongue. All eyes. Be silent.

[*Enter* Iris.]

60 **Iris.** Ceres, most bounteous lady, thy rich leas
Of wheat, rye, barley, vetches, oats, and peas;
Thy turfy mountains, where live nibbling sheep,
And flat meads thatched with stover, them to keep;
Thy banks with pionèd and twillèd brims,
65   Which spongy April at thy hest betrims
To make cold nymphs chaste crowns; and thy
    broom groves,
Whose shadow the dismissèd bachelor loves,
Being lass-lorn; thy poll-clipped vineyard,
And thy sea marge, sterile and rocky hard,
70   Where thou thyself dost air—the Queen o' th' sky,
Whose wat'ry arch and messenger am I,
Bids thee leave these, and with her sovereign grace,
Here on this grass-plot, in this very place,
To come and sport. Her peacocks fly amain.
75   Approach, rich Ceres, her to entertain.

[*Enter* Ceres.]

Ceres. Hail, many-colored messenger, that ne'er
    Dost disobey the wife of Jupiter;

81 ***bosky:*** covered with bushes; ***unshrubbed down:*** bare plain.

85 ***estate:*** bestow.

86 ***bow:*** rainbow.
87 ***her son:*** the blind Cupid.

89 ***Dis:*** Pluto, god of the underworld, who abducted Ceres' daughter Proserpina after being struck by Cupid's arrow.
90 ***scandaled:*** scandalous.

94 ***Dove-drawn:*** Venus's chariot was drawn by doves.
94–95 ***done . . . charm:*** cast a lewd spell.
96 ***bed-right:*** right to consummate the marriage.
97 ***Till . . . lighted:*** until the wedding ceremony is performed.
98 ***Mars's hot minion:*** Venus, lover of the Roman god of war.
99 ***waspish-headed:*** peevish.

101 ***right out:*** entirely.

       Who with thy saffron wings upon my flowers
       Diffusest honey drops, refreshing showers;
80   And with each end of thy blue bow dost crown
       My bosky acres and my unshrubbed down,
       Rich scarf to my proud earth. Why hath thy queen
       Summoned me hither to this short-grassed green?

Iris. A contract of true love to celebrate,
85   And some donation freely to estate
       On the blest lovers.

Ceres.   Tell me, heavenly bow,
       If Venus or her son, as thou dost know,
       Do now attend the Queen? Since they did plot
       The means that dusky Dis my daughter got,
90   Her and her blind boy's scandaled company
       I have forsworn.

Iris.   Of her society
       Be not afraid. I met her deity
       Cutting the clouds towards Paphos, and her son
       Dove-drawn with her. Here thought they to have done
95   Some wanton charm upon this man and maid,
       Whose vows are that no bed-right shall be paid
       Till Hymen's torch be lighted—but in vain.
       Mars's hot minion is returned again;
       Her waspish-headed son has broke his arrows,
100 Swears he will shoot no more, but play with sparrows,
       And be a boy right out.

[Juno *descends.*]

Ceres.   Highest queen of state,
       Great Juno comes. I know her by her gait.

Juno. How does my bounteous sister? Go with me
       To bless this twain, that they may prosperous be
105 And honored in their issue.

[*They sing.*]

108 ***still:*** always.

110 ***foison:*** abundance.
111 ***garners:*** grain bins.

114–115 ***Spring . . . harvest:*** May spring arrive no later than the end of autumn (thus eliminating winter).

119 ***May I be bold:*** would I be correct.

121 ***confines:*** region.

128 ***naiads:*** water nymphs; ***wind'ring:*** winding; wandering.
129 ***sedged crowns:*** garlands of reeds.
130 ***crisp:*** rippling.

Juno. *Honor, riches, marriage-blessing,*
Long continuance, and increasing,
Hourly joys be still upon you.
Juno sings her blessings on you.

110 **Ceres.** *Earth's increase, foison plenty,*
Barns and garners never empty,
Vines with clust'ring bunches growing,
Plants with goodly burden bowing;
Spring come to you at the farthest
115 *In the very end of harvest.*
Scarcity and want shall shun you.
Ceres' blessing so is on you.

Ferdinand. This is a most majestic vision, and
Harmonious charmingly. May I be bold
120 To think these spirits?

Prospero. Spirits, which by mine art
I have from their confines called to enact
My present fancies.

Ferdinand. Let me live here ever.
So rare a wondered father and a wife
Makes this place paradise.

[*Juno and Ceres whisper, and send* Iris *on employment.*]

Prospero. Sweet now, silence.
125 Juno and Ceres whisper seriously.
There's something else to do. Hush, and be mute,
Or else our spell is marred.

Iris. You nymphs, called naiads of the windring brooks,
With your sedged crowns and ever-harmless looks,
130 Leave your crisp channels and on this green land
Answer your summons, Juno does command.
Come, temperate nymphs, and help to celebrate
A contract of true love. Be not too late.

[*Enter certain* Nymphs.]

134 *sicklemen:* harvesters.
135 *furrow:* plowed field.

137 *encounter:* come together.
138 *footing:* dancing.
Stage direction—*habited:* dressed.

142 *Avoid:* go away.

144 *works:* agitates.

145 *distempered:* disturbed.

146 *moved sort:* troubled state.

148 *revels:* entertainment.
149 *foretold you:* told you before.

151 *baseless fabric:* structure without a foundation.

154 *all which it inherit:* all who come to possess it.

156 *rack:* mist (trace).
157 *on:* of.
158 *rounded:* rounded off.

You sunburned sicklemen, of August weary,
135   Come hither from the furrow and be merry.
Make holiday: your rye-straw hats put on,
And these fresh nymphs encounter every one
In country footing.

[*Enter certain* Reapers, *properly habited. They join with
the* Nymphs *in a graceful dance, towards the end whereof*
Prospero *starts suddenly and speaks.*]

Prospero. I had forgot that foul conspiracy
140   Of the beast Caliban and his confederates
Against my life. The minute of their plot
Is almost come.—Well done. Avoid. No more.

[*To a strange, hollow, and confused noise, the spirits
heavily vanish.*]

Ferdinand [*to* Miranda]. This is strange. Your father's in
    some passion
That works him strongly.

Miranda.   Never till this day
145   Saw I him touched with anger, so distempered.

Prospero [*to* Ferdinand]. You do look, my son, in a
    moved sort,
As if you were dismayed. Be cheerful, sir.
Our revels now are ended. These our actors,
As I foretold you, were all spirits and
150   Are melted into air, into thin air;
And like the baseless fabric of this vision,
The cloud-capped towers, the gorgeous palaces,
The solemn temples, the great globe itself,
Yea, all which it inherit, shall dissolve,
155   And, like this insubstantial pageant faded,
Leave not a rack behind. We are such stuff
As dreams are made on, and our little life
Is rounded with a sleep. Sir, I am vexed.
Bear with my weakness. My old brain is troubled.
160   Be not disturbed with my infirmity.

164 *with a thought:* in an instant.

167 *presented:* acted or introduced.

170 *varlets:* rascals.

172 *smote:* struck.

174 *bending:* aiming.

176 *unbacked:* unbroken.
177 *Advanced:* raised.
178 *As:* as if.
179 *lowing:* mooing.
180 *briers . . . furzes . . . gorse:* types of thorny shrubs.

182 *filthy-mantled:* scum-covered.
183 *that:* so that.
184 *O'erstunk:* stunk worse than.

If you be pleased, retire into my cell
And there repose. A turn or two I'll walk
To still my beating mind.

Ferdinand and Miranda.   We wish your peace.

[*They exit.*]

[*Enter* Ariel.]

Prospero. Come with a thought. I thank thee, Ariel.
   Come.

165 **Ariel.** Thy thoughts I cleave to. What's thy pleasure?

Prospero.   Spirit,
   We must prepare to meet with Caliban.

Ariel. Ay, my commander. When I presented Ceres,
   I thought to have told thee of it, but I feared
   Lest I might anger thee.

170 **Prospero.** Say again, where didst thou leave these varlets?

Ariel. I told you, sir, they were red-hot with drinking,
   So full of valor that they smote the air
   For breathing in their faces, beat the ground
   For kissing of their feet; yet always bending
175   Towards their project. Then I beat my tabor,
   At which, like unbacked colts, they pricked their ears,
   Advanced their eyelids, lifted up their noses
   As they smelt music. So I charmed their ears
   That, calf-like, they my lowing followed through
180   Toothed briers, sharp furzes, pricking gorse, and
      thorns,
   Which entered their frail shins. At last I left them
   I' th' filthy-mantled pool beyond your cell,
   There dancing up to th' chins, that the foul lake
   O'erstunk their feet.

Prospero.   This was well done, my bird.
185   Thy shape invisible retain thou still.

186 *trumpery:* worthless finery.
187 *stale:* decoy.

189 *Nurture:* education.

192 *cankers:* grows increasingly corrupt.

193 *line:* lime (linden) tree.

197–198 *played the jack with us:* made fools of us.

199 *smell all:* smell entirely of.

206 *hoodwink this mischance:* make this misfortune harmless.

> The trumpery in my house, go bring it hither
> For stale to catch these thieves.
>
> **Ariel.**   I go, I go.
>
> [*He exits.*]
>
> **Prospero.** A devil, a born devil, on whose nature
> Nurture can never stick; on whom my pains,
> Humanely taken, all, all lost, quite lost;
> And as with age his body uglier grows,
> So his mind cankers. I will plague them all
> Even to roaring.
>
> [*Enter* Ariel, *loaden with glistering apparel, etc.*]
>
>   Come, hang them on this line.
>
> [*Enter* Caliban, Stephano, *and* Trinculo, *all wet, as* Prospero *and* Ariel *look on.*]
>
> **Caliban.** Pray you, tread softly, that the blind mole
> may not hear a footfall. We now are near his cell.
>
> **Stephano.** Monster, your fairy, which you say is a
> harmless fairy, has done little better than played the
> jack with us.
>
> **Trinculo.** Monster, I do smell all horse piss, at which
> my nose is in great indignation.
>
> **Stephano.** So is mine.—Do you hear, monster. If I
> should take a displeasure against you, look you—
>
> **Trinculo.** Thou wert but a lost monster.
>
> **Caliban.** Good my lord, give me thy favor still.
> Be patient, for the prize I'll bring thee to
> Shall hoodwink this mischance. Therefore speak
>   softly.
> All's hushed as midnight yet.
>
> **Trinculo.** Ay, but to lose our bottles in the pool!

213 *fetch off:* rescue.
213–214 *o'er ears:* drowned.

219 *For aye:* forever.

227 *frippery:* old-clothes shop. *What point do you think Trinculo is making with this remark?*

232 *dropsy:* a disease that causes fluid to build up in the body.
233 *luggage:* something that must be lugged around.

237 *Mistress Line:* the lime tree.
238 *jerkin:* close-fitting jacket.
239 *under the line:* taken off the lime tree (with a play on the meaning "at the equator," where travelers often caught fevers that caused their hair to fall out).

Stephano. There is not only disgrace and dishonor in
210   that, monster, but an infinite loss.

Trinculo. That's more to me than my wetting. Yet this is
your harmless fairy, monster!

Stephano. I will fetch off my bottle, though I be o'er
ears for my labor.

215 **Caliban.** Prithee, my king, be quiet. Seest thou here,
This is the mouth o' th' cell. No noise, and enter.
Do that good mischief which may make this island
Thine own forever, and I, thy Caliban,
For aye thy foot-licker.

220 **Stephano.** Give me thy hand. I do begin to have bloody
thoughts.

Trinculo [*seeing the apparel*]. O King Stephano, O peer,
O worthy Stephano, look what a wardrobe here is
for thee!

225 **Caliban.** Let it alone, thou fool. It is but trash.

Trinculo. Oho, monster, we know what belongs to a
frippery. [*He puts on one of the gowns.*] O King
Stephano!

Stephano. Put off that gown, Trinculo. By this hand,
230   I'll have that gown.

Trinculo. Thy Grace shall have it.

Caliban. The dropsy drown this fool! What do you mean
To dote thus on such luggage? Let 't alone,
And do the murder first. If he awake,
235 From toe to crown he'll fill our skins with pinches,
Make us strange stuff.

Stephano. Be you quiet, monster.—Mistress Line, is not
this my jerkin? [*He takes a jacket from the tree.*] Now
is the jerkin under the line.—Now, jerkin, you are
240   like to lose your hair and prove a bald jerkin.

241 *by line and level:* by the rules; *an 't like:* if it please.

246 *pass of pate:* clever thrust.
247–248 *put . . . fingers:* be sticky-fingered.

251 *villainous:* wretchedly.
252 *lay to:* apply.

Stage direction—*divers:* various.

257–259 *Mountain . . . Silver . . . Fury . . . Tyrant:* dog names.

260 *charge:* order.

262 *pinch-spotted:* bruised from pinches.

263 *pard or cat o' mountain:* leopard or panther.

Trinculo. Do, do. We steal by line and level, an 't like your Grace.

Stephano. I thank thee for that jest. Here's a garment for 't. Wit shall not go unrewarded while I am king of this country. "Steal by line and level" is an excellent pass of pate. There's another garment for 't.

Trinculo. Monster, come, put some lime upon your fingers, and away with the rest.

Caliban. I will have none on 't. We shall lose our time
And all be turned to barnacles or to apes
With foreheads villainous low.

Stephano. Monster, lay to your fingers. Help to bear this away where my hogshead of wine is, or I'll turn you out of my kingdom. Go to, carry this.

Trinculo. And this.

Stephano. Ay, and this.

[*a noise of hunters heard*]

[*Enter divers spirits in shape of dogs and hounds, hunting them about,* Prospero *and* Ariel *setting them on.*]

Prospero. Hey, Mountain, hey!

Ariel. Silver! There it goes, Silver!

Prospero. Fury, Fury! There, Tyrant, there! Hark, hark!

[Caliban, Stephano, *and* Trinculo *are driven off.*]

Go, charge my goblins that they grind their joints
With dry convulsions, shorten up their sinews
With agèd cramps, and more pinch-spotted make them
Than pard or cat o' mountain.

Ariel.   Hark, they roar.

Prospero. Let them be hunted soundly. At this hour
Lies at my mercy all mine enemies.
Shortly shall all my labors end, and thou
Shalt have the air at freedom. For a little
Follow and do me service.

[*They exit.*]

1 ***project:*** scheme; ***gather to a head:*** come to a boil.

3 ***Goes . . . carriage:*** walks without stooping (because his burden is light).

7 ***and 's:*** and his.

8 ***gave in charge:*** commanded.

10 ***weather-fends:*** protects from the weather.
11 ***your release:*** you release them.
12 ***abide:*** remain; ***distracted:*** deranged.

17 ***eaves of reeds:*** thatched roofs.

18 ***affections:*** feelings.

ACT FIVE

Scene 1

[*Enter* Prospero *in his magic robes, and* Ariel.]

Prospero. Now does my project gather to a head.
My charms crack not, my spirits obey, and time
Goes upright with his carriage.—How's the day?

Ariel. On the sixth hour, at which time, my lord,
5   You said our work should cease.

Prospero.   I did say so
When first I raised the tempest. Say, my spirit,
How fares the King and 's followers?

Ariel.   Confined together
In the same fashion as you gave in charge,
Just as you left them; all prisoners, sir,
10   In the line grove which weather-fends your cell.
They cannot budge till your release. The King,
His brother, and yours abide all three distracted,
And the remainder mourning over them,
Brimful of sorrow and dismay; but chiefly
15   Him that you termed, sir, the good old Lord Gonzalo.
His tears runs down his beard like winter's drops
From eaves of reeds. Your charm so strongly
     works 'em
That if you now beheld them, your affections
Would become tender.

Prospero.   Dost thou think so, spirit?

20 **Ariel.** Mine would, sir, were I human.

Prospero.   And mine shall.
Hast thou, which art but air, a touch, a feeling

The Tempest   139

23–24 *that relish . . . they:* who feels suffering as keenly as they do.
24 *kindlier:* more generously.

29 *The sole drift of my purpose:* my sole intention.

35 *ebbing Neptune:* retreating tide; *fly:* flee from.
36 *demi-puppets:* semi-puppets.
37 *green sour ringlets:* fairy rings (circles of sour grass).

39 *midnight mushrumps:* mushrooms that appear overnight; *that:* you who.
40 *solemn curfew:* the evening bell (which marks the hour when spirits are free to roam).
41 *masters:* agents; instruments.
43 *azured vault:* blue sky.

45 *rifted:* split; *oak:* a tree sacred to Jove (Jupiter), the Roman god of thunder.
46 *bolt:* thunderbolt.
47 *spurs:* roots.

51 *abjure:* renounce; *required:* requested.

Of their afflictions, and shall not myself,
One of their kind, that relish all as sharply
Passion as they, be kindlier moved than thou art?
Though with their high wrongs I am struck to th' quick,
Yet with my nobler reason 'gainst my fury
Do I take part. The rarer action is
In virtue than in vengeance. They being penitent,
The sole drift of my purpose doth extend
Not a frown further. Go, release them, Ariel.
My charms I'll break, their senses I'll restore,
And they shall be themselves.

Ariel.   I'll fetch them, sir.

[*He exits.*]

[Prospero *draws a large circle on the stage with his staff.*]

Prospero. You elves of hills, brooks, standing lakes, and groves,
And you that on the sands with printless foot
Do chase the ebbing Neptune, and do fly him
When he comes back; you demi-puppets that
By moonshine do the green sour ringlets make,
Whereof the ewe not bites; and you whose pastime
Is to make midnight mushrumps, that rejoice
To hear the solemn curfew; by whose aid,
Weak masters though you be, I have bedimmed
The noontide sun, called forth the mutinous winds,
And 'twixt the green sea and the azured vault
Set roaring war; to the dread rattling thunder
Have I given fire, and rifted Jove's stout oak
With his own bolt; the strong-based promontory
Have I made shake, and by the spurs plucked up
The pine and cedar; graves at my command
Have waked their sleepers, oped, and let 'em forth
By my so potent art. But this rough magic
I here abjure, and when I have required
Some heavenly music, which even now I do,

53–54 ***their senses . . . for:*** the senses of those whom this music is for.

56 ***plummet:*** a weight attached to a line; ***sound:*** measure depth.

58 ***air:*** tune; ***and:*** which is.

63–64 ***Mine eyes . . . drops:*** my eyes, sympathetic to the sight of your weeping, shed tears as well.

67 ***ignorant fumes:*** fogs of ignorance; ***mantle:*** cover.
68 ***clearer:*** growing clearer.
69 ***sir:*** gentleman.
70–71 ***pay . . . home:*** fully repay your favors.

73 ***furtherer:*** accomplice.
74 ***pinched:*** tormented.

76 ***remorse and nature:*** pity and natural feelings for a brother; ***whom:*** who.
77 ***inward pinches:*** guilt.

[Prospero *gestures with his staff.*]

> To work mine end upon their senses that
> This airy charm is for, I'll break my staff,
> Bury it certain fathoms in the earth,
> And deeper than did ever plummet sound
> I'll drown my book.

[*solemn music*]

[Here enters Ariel *before; then* Alonso *with a frantic gesture, attended by* Gonzalo; Sebastian *and* Antonio *in like manner attended by* Adrian *and* Francisco. *They all enter the circle which* Prospero *had made, and there stand charmed; which* Prospero *observing, speaks.*]

> A solemn air, and the best comforter
> To an unsettled fancy, cure thy brains,
> Now useless, boiled within thy skull. There stand,
> For you are spell-stopped.—
> Holy Gonzalo, honorable man,
> Mine eyes, e'en sociable to the show of thine,
> Fall fellowly drops.—The charm dissolves apace,
> And as the morning steals upon the night,
> Melting the darkness, so their rising senses
> Begin to chase the ignorant fumes that mantle
> Their clearer reason.—O good Gonzalo,
> My true preserver and a loyal sir
> To him thou follow'st, I will pay thy graces
> Home, both in word and deed.—Most cruelly
> Didst thou, Alonso, use me and my daughter.
> Thy brother was a furtherer in the act.—
> Thou art pinched for 't now, Sebastian.—Flesh and blood,
> You, brother mine, that entertained ambition,
> Expelled remorse and nature, whom, with Sebastian,
> Whose inward pinches therefore are most strong,
> Would here have killed your king, I do forgive thee,
> Unnatural though thou art.—Their understanding
> Begins to swell, and the approaching tide
> Will shortly fill the reasonable shore

84 *rapier:* sword (which Prospero would have worn as an aristocrat).

85 *discase me:* remove my magic robes.
86 *sometime Milan:* formerly, when duke of Milan.

101 *presently:* immediately.

103 *Or ere:* before.

That now lies foul and muddy. Not one of them
That yet looks on me, or would know me.—Ariel,
Fetch me the hat and rapier in my cell.

[Ariel *exits and at once returns with Prospero's ducal robes.*]

85 I will discase me and myself present
As I was sometime Milan.—Quickly, spirit,
Thou shalt ere long be free.

Ariel [*sings, and helps to attire him*].
    Where the bee sucks, there suck I.
    In a cowslip's bell I lie.
90   *There I couch when owls do cry.*
    On the bat's back I do fly
    After summer merrily.
    Merrily, merrily shall I live now
    Under the blossom that hangs on the bow.

95 **Prospero.** Why, that's my dainty Ariel. I shall miss
Thee, but yet thou shalt have freedom. So, so, so.
To the King's ship, invisible as thou art.
There shalt thou find the mariners asleep
Under the hatches. The master and the boatswain
100 Being awake, enforce them to this place,
And presently, I prithee.

Ariel. I drink the air before me, and return
Or ere your pulse twice beat.

[*He exits.*]

Gonzalo. All torment, trouble, wonder, and amazement
105 Inhabits here. Some heavenly power guide us
Out of this fearful country!

Prospero [*to* Alonso].   Behold, sir king,
The wrongèd Duke of Milan, Prospero.
For more assurance that a living prince
Does now speak to thee, I embrace thy body,

[*He embraces* Alonso.]

111 ***Whe'er:*** whether; ***no:*** not.
112 ***trifle:*** illusion; ***abuse:*** deceive.
113 ***late:*** lately.

116–117 ***This must . . . story:*** This would require, if it is really happening, a strange explanation.
118 ***Thy dukedom:*** my right to tribute from your dukedom.

121 ***age:*** aged self.
122 ***confined:*** limited.

124 ***subtleties:*** illusions.

126 ***brace:*** pair.

128 ***justify:*** prove.

134 ***perforce:*** of necessity.

110   And to thee and thy company I bid
A hearty welcome.

Alonso.   Whe'er thou be'st he or no,
Or some enchanted trifle to abuse me
(As late I have been) I not know. Thy pulse
Beats as of flesh and blood; and since I saw thee,
115   Th' affliction of my mind amends, with which
I fear a madness held me. This must crave,
An if this be at all, a most strange story.
Thy dukedom I resign, and do entreat
Thou pardon me my wrongs. But how should Prospero
120   Be living and be here?

Prospero [*to* Gonzalo].   First, noble friend,
Let me embrace thine age, whose honor cannot
Be measured or confined.

Gonzalo.   Whether this be
Or be not, I'll not swear.

Prospero.   You do yet taste
Some subtleties o' th' isle, that will not let you
125   Believe things certain. Welcome, my friends all.

[*aside to* Sebastian *and* Antonio]

But you, my brace of lords, were I so minded,
I here could pluck his Highness' frown upon you
And justify you traitors. At this time
I will tell no tales.

Sebastian [*aside*].   The devil speaks in him.

130 **Prospero** [*aside to* Sebastian]. No.
[*to* Antonio] For you, most wicked sir, whom to call brother
Would even infect my mouth, I do forgive
Thy rankest fault, all of them, and require
My dukedom of thee, which perforce I know
135   Thou must restore.

137 ***whom:*** who.

140 ***woe:*** sorry.

143 ***of whose soft grace:*** by whose mercy.
144 ***the like:*** a similar.

146 ***as late:*** as it is recent.
146–148 ***supportable . . . comfort you:*** I have much weaker means to make the grievous loss bearable than you have to comfort yourself. *In what sense has Prospero really "lost" Miranda?*

153 ***mudded:*** buried.

156 ***admire:*** wonder.
157–159 ***scarce think . . . breath:*** hardly believe that their eyes function properly or that their words are human speech.

Alonso. If thou be'st Prospero,
Give us particulars of thy preservation,
How thou hast met us here, whom three hours since
Were wracked upon this shore, where I have lost—
How sharp the point of this remembrance is!—
140   My dear son Ferdinand.

Prospero. I am woe for 't, sir.

Alonso. Irreparable is the loss, and patience
Says it is past her cure.

Prospero. I rather think
You have not sought her help, of whose soft grace,
For the like loss, I have her sovereign aid
145   And rest myself content.

Alonso. You the like loss?

Prospero. As great to me as late, and supportable
To make the dear loss have I means much weaker
Than you may call to comfort you, for I
Have lost my daughter.

150 **Alonso.** A daughter?
O heavens, that they were living both in Naples,
The King and Queen there! That they were, I wish
Myself were mudded in that oozy bed
Where my son lies!—When did you lose your
  daughter?

155 **Prospero.** In this last tempest. I perceive these lords
At this encounter do so much admire
That they devour their reason, and scarce think
Their eyes do offices of truth, their words
Are natural breath.—But howsoe'er you have
160   Been justled from your senses, know for certain
That I am Prospero and that very duke
Which was thrust forth of Milan, who most strangely
Upon this shore, where you were wracked, was
  landed
To be the lord on 't. No more yet of this,

165 ***chronicle of day by day:*** story to be told over days.
166 ***relation:*** account.

169 ***abroad:*** elsewhere.

Stage directions—***discovers:*** reveals by drawing back a curtain.

174 ***play me false:*** are cheating me.

176–177 ***Yes, for a score . . . play:*** Yes, you did, and if you tried to win 20 kingdoms from me (not just this chess game), I would let you get away with it.

178 ***vision:*** illusion.

182 ***compass:*** encircle.

165   For 'tis a chronicle of day by day,
           Not a relation for a breakfast, nor
           Befitting this first meeting. [*to* Alonso] Welcome, sir.
           This cell's my court. Here have I few attendants,
           And subjects none abroad. Pray you, look in.
170   My dukedom since you have given me again,
           I will requite you with as good a thing,
           At least bring forth a wonder to content you
           As much as me my dukedom.

[*Here* Prospero *discovers* Ferdinand *and* Miranda, *playing at chess.*]

Miranda [*to* Ferdinand].
   Sweet lord, you play me false.

Ferdinand.   No, my dearest love,
175   I would not for the world.

Miranda. Yes, for a score of kingdoms you should wrangle,
   And I would call it fair play.

Alonso.   If this prove
   A vision of the island, one dear son
   Shall I twice lose.

Sebastian.   A most high miracle!

Ferdinand [*seeing* Alonso *and coming forward*].
180   Though the seas threaten, they are merciful.
        I have cursed them without cause.

[*He kneels.*]

Alonso.   Now, all the blessings
   Of a glad father compass thee about!
   Arise, and say how thou cam'st here.

[Ferdinand *stands.*]

Miranda [*rising and coming* forward].   O wonder!
   How many goodly creatures are there here!

185 brave: excellent; admirable.
186 *What do you think Prospero is suggesting about Miranda?*

188 eld'st: longest.

198 I am hers: I am her second father.

202 inly: inwardly.

205 chalked forth: marked out.

207 Milan thrust from Milan: the duke of Milan forced out of his city; **issue:** descendants. *What point is Gonzalo making with this question?*

		How beauteous mankind is! O, brave new world
		That has such people in 't!

	Prospero. 'Tis new to thee.

	Alonso [*to* Ferdinand]. What is this maid with whom
			thou wast at play?
		Your eld'st acquaintance cannot be three hours.
		Is she the goddess that hath severed us
		And brought us thus together?

	Ferdinand. Sir, she is mortal,
		But by immortal providence she's mine.
		I chose her when I could not ask my father
		For his advice, nor thought I had one. She
		Is daughter to this famous Duke of Milan,
		Of whom so often I have heard renown,
		But never saw before, of whom I have
		Received a second life; and second father
		This lady makes him to me.

	Alonso. I am hers.
		But, O, how oddly will it sound that I
		Must ask my child forgiveness!

	Prospero. There, sir, stop.
		Let us not burden our remembrances with
		A heaviness that's gone.

	Gonzalo. I have inly wept
		Or should have spoke ere this. Look down, you gods,
		And on this couple drop a blessèd crown,
		For it is you that have chalked forth the way
		Which brought us hither.

	Alonso. I say "Amen," Gonzalo.

	Gonzalo. Was Milan thrust from Milan, that his issue
		Should become kings of Naples? O, rejoice
		Beyond a common joy, and set it down
		With gold on lasting pillars: in one voyage
		Did Claribel her husband find at Tunis,

The Tempest

215 ***his own:*** himself.

216–217 ***still embrace . . . That:*** always embrace the heart of anyone who.

220 ***blasphemy:*** blasphemer.

225 ***Which . . . split:*** which only three hours ago we declared split.
226 ***tight and yare:*** watertight and seaworthy.

228 ***tricksy:*** clever.
229 ***strengthen:*** increase.

232 ***dead of sleep:*** sound asleep.
233 ***clapped:*** shut away.
234 ***several:*** various.

238 ***in all her trim:*** fully rigged and ready to sail.

And Ferdinand, her brother, found a wife
Where he himself was lost; Prospero his dukedom
In a poor isle; and all of us ourselves
When no man was his own.

Alonso [*to* Ferdinand *and* Miranda]. Give me your hands.
Let grief and sorrow still embrace his heart
That doth not wish you joy!

Gonzalo.   Be it so. Amen.

[*Enter* Ariel, *with the* Master *and* Boatswain *amazedly following.*]

O, look, sir, look, sir, here is more of us.
I prophesied if a gallows were on land,
This fellow could not drown. Now, blasphemy,
That swear'st grace o'erboard, not an oath on shore?
Hast thou no mouth by land? What is the news?

Boatswain. The best news is that we have safely found
Our king and company. The next: our ship,
Which, but three glasses since, we gave out split,
Is tight and yare and bravely rigged as when
We first put out to sea.

Ariel [*aside to* Prospero].   Sir, all this service
Have I done since I went.

Prospero [*aside to* Ariel].   My tricksy spirit!

Alonso. These are not natural events. They strengthen
From strange to stranger.—Say, how came you hither?

Boatswain. If I did think, sir, I were well awake,
I'd strive to tell you. We were dead of sleep
And—how, we know not—all clapped under hatches,
Where, but even now, with strange and several noises
Of roaring, shrieking, howling, jingling chains,
And more diversity of sounds, all horrible,
We were awaked, straightway at liberty,
Where we, in all her trim, freshly beheld
Our royal, good, and gallant ship, our master

The Tempest

240 Cap'ring to eye her: dancing for joy upon seeing her;
On a trice: in an instant.

242 moping: dazed.

246 conduct: conductor; director.

248 Do not . . . on: do not trouble your mind with continual worry about.
249 picked leisure: a convenient time of our choice.
250–252 single . . . accidents: I alone will provide you with a convincing explanation of all the events that have occurred.

258 shift for all the rest: take care of everyone else (a drunken reversal of the expression "Every man shift for himself").

260 Coraggio, bully monster: Courage, excellent monster.

261 true spies: trustworthy observers (eyes).

264 fine: splendidly dressed.

240 Cap'ring to eye her. On a trice, so please you,
Even in a dream were we divided from them
And were brought moping hither.

Ariel [*aside to* Prospero].   Was 't well done?

Prospero [*aside to* Ariel]. Bravely, my diligence. Thou
shalt be free.

Alonso. This is as strange a maze as e'er men trod,
245 And there is in this business more than nature
Was ever conduct of. Some oracle
Must rectify our knowledge.

Prospero.   Sir, my liege,
Do not infest your mind with beating on
The strangeness of this business. At picked leisure,
250 Which shall be shortly, single I'll resolve you,
Which to you shall seem probable, of every
These happened accidents; till when, be cheerful
And think of each thing well. [*aside to* Ariel] Come
   hither, spirit;
Set Caliban and his companions free.
255 Untie the spell. [*Ariel exits.*] How fares my gracious sir?
There are yet missing of your company
Some few odd lads that you remember not.

[*Enter* Ariel, *driving in* Caliban, Stephano, *and* Trinculo *in their stolen apparel.*]

Stephano. Every man shift for all the rest, and let no
man take care for himself, for all is but fortune.
260 Coraggio, bully monster, coraggio.

Trinculo. If these be true spies which I wear in my head,
here's a goodly sight.

Caliban. O Setebos, these be brave spirits indeed! How
fine my master is! I am afraid he will chastise me.

265 **Sebastian.** Ha, ha!
What things are these, my Lord Antonio?
Will money buy 'em?

267 **like:** likely.

269 **Mark:** notice; **badges:** emblems worn by servants to identify which houses they belonged to.

273 **deal . . . power:** exercise the moon's authority outside of her control.
274 **demi-devil:** half-devil.

277 **own:** acknowledge to be yours.

281 **reeling ripe:** drunk enough to be reeling.
282 **gilded 'em:** made their faces flushed.

286 **not fear flyblowing:** not fear being infested by flies like rotten meat (since he is preserved by pickling).

290 **sirrah:** a term used to address an inferior.

296 **trim:** prepare.

Antonio. Very like. One of them
Is a plain fish and no doubt marketable.

Prospero. Mark but the badges of these men, my lords,
Then say if they be true. This misshapen knave,
His mother was a witch, and one so strong
That could control the moon, make flows and ebbs,
And deal in her command without her power.
These three have robbed me, and this demi-devil,
For he's a bastard one, had plotted with them
To take my life. Two of these fellows you
Must know and own. This thing of darkness I
Acknowledge mine.

Caliban. I shall be pinched to death.

Alonso. Is not this Stephano, my drunken butler?

Sebastian. He is drunk now. Where had he wine?

Alonso. And Trinculo is reeling ripe. Where should they
Find this grand liquor that hath gilded 'em?
[*to* Trinculo] How cam'st thou in this pickle?

Trinculo. I have been in such a pickle since I saw you
last that I fear me will never out of my bones. I
shall not fear flyblowing.

Sebastian. Why, how now, Stephano?

Stephano. O, touch me not! I am not Stephano, but
a cramp.

Prospero. You'd be king o' the isle, sirrah?

Stephano. I should have been a sore one, then.

Alonso [*indicating* Caliban]. This is as strange a thing as
e'er I looked on.

Prospero. He is as disproportioned in his manners
As in his shape. [*to* Caliban] Go, sirrah, to my cell.
Take with you your companions. As you look
To have my pardon, trim it handsomely.

298 *grace:* pardon.

301 *luggage:* the stolen clothes.

305 *which part . . . waste:* part of which I'll occupy.

308 *accidents:* events.

311–312 *the nuptial . . . solemnized:* the marriage of our loved ones properly celebrated.

314 *shall be my grave:* shall be about my mortality.

316 *Take:* captivate; *deliver all:* report everything.

317 *auspicious gales:* favorable winds.
318–319 *so expeditious . . . off:* so speedy that we shall catch up to your distant royal fleet.

321 *draw near:* go in.

Caliban. Ay, that I will, and I'll be wise hereafter
And seek for grace. What a thrice-double ass
Was I to take this drunkard for a god,
300 And worship this dull fool!

Prospero. Go to, away!

Alonso [*to* Stephano *and* Trinculo]. Hence, and bestow
your luggage where you found it.

Sebastian. Or stole it, rather.

[Caliban, Stephano, *and* Trinculo *exit.*]

Prospero. Sir, I invite your Highness and your train
To my poor cell, where you shall take your rest
305 For this one night, which part of it I'll waste
With such discourse as, I not doubt, shall make it
Go quick away: the story of my life
And the particular accidents gone by
Since I came to this isle. And in the morn
310 I'll bring you to your ship, and so to Naples,
Where I have hope to see the nuptial
Of these our dear-belovèd solemnized,
And thence retire me to my Milan, where
Every third thought shall be my grave.

Alonso. I long
315 To hear the story of your life, which must
Take the ear strangely.

Prospero. I'll deliver all,
And promise you calm seas, auspicious gales,
And sail so expeditious that shall catch
Your royal fleet far off. [*aside to* Ariel] My Ariel, chick,
320 That is thy charge. Then to the elements
Be free, and fare thou well.—Please you, draw near.

[*They all exit.*]

9 ***bands:*** bonds.
10 ***good hands:*** applause.
11 ***Gentle breath:*** kind words.

13 ***want:*** lack.

15–16 ***my ending . . . prayer:*** this performance will be a failure unless you respond to my plea for your approval.

18 ***frees:*** frees one from.

20 ***indulgence:*** pardon (in the form of applause).

EPILOGUE, *spoken by Prospero*

    Now my charms are all o'erthrown,
    And what strength I have 's mine own,
    Which is most faint. Now 'tis true
    I must be here confined by you,
5 Or sent to Naples. Let me not,
    Since I have my dukedom got
    And pardoned the deceiver, dwell
    In this bare island by your spell,
    But release me from my bands
10 With the help of your good hands.
    Gentle breath of yours my sails
    Must fill, or else my project fails,
    Which was to please. Now I want
    Spirits to enforce, art to enchant,
15 And my ending is despair,
    Unless I be relieved by prayer,
    Which pierces so that it assaults
    Mercy itself, and frees all faults.
    As you from crimes would pardoned be,
20 Let your indulgence set me free.

    [*He exits.*]

Related Readings

CONTENTS

The Tempest
What insights can we gather from Shakespeare's last play?
essay by Norrie Epstein   169

***from* A True Reportory of the Wreck and Redemption of Sir Thomas Gates, Knight**
A witness attests to a disastrous storm.
historical account by William Strachey   176

The Sire de Malétroit's Door
What makes two people fall in love?
short story by Robert Louis Stevenson   181

Rappaccini's Daughter
Love baits an unsuspecting victim.
short story by Nathaniel Hawthorne   206

Caliban
A modern take on this unusual character
essay by Norrie Epstein   242

***from* A Tempest**
How do Prospero, Caliban, and Ariel really feel about each other?
drama by Aimé Cesaire   245

I Will Come Back
Leaving one's mark on the world
poem by Pablo Neruda   251

Related Readings

The Tempest

by Norrie Epstein

The Tempest is a play that can be enjoyed on many different levels. In the following essay, critic Norrie Epstein offers help in interpreting Shakespeare's last play.

The Tempest begins in the middle of a shipwreck. Certain of death, men scream out against the roar of waves crashing, while overhead, lightning streaks the sky. This is one of the most gripping opening scenes Shakespeare ever wrote, as if more than ever he wanted to draw his audience into the dramatic action one last time. By the end of the scene, it seems the men have drowned, and the audience feels as if they, too, have been through an ordeal. Yet with its extravagant effects, the scene, unlike Shakespeare's usual muted beginnings, calls attention to itself as theatre. We are drawn into the tumult while at the same time we marvel at the stagecraft needed to create the illusion.

These two perspectives—one engaged, one distant—are mirrored in the next scene: from on shore, Miranda watches the shipwreck, and although her father allays her fears, assuring her that "there's no harm done," she weeps for the drowning men. Prospero serenely observes the disaster (which he calls a "spectacle"), his perspective one of god-like detachment, secure in the knowledge that the men are safe. Suddenly we realize, as we have suspected all along, that we've been duped; what seemed so realistic and thrilling turns out to be an illusion of an illusion, Prospero's magic, analogous to theatrical sleight of hand. Both magician and playwright seem to manipulate nature, bringing forth objects out of "thin air," making us believe in a reality without substance. Throughout *The Tempest* Shakespeare continually reminds us that we are watching transient shadows:

> Our revels now are ended. These our actors,
> As I foretold you, were all spirits, and
> Are melted into air, into thin air;
> And, like the baseless fabric of this vision,
> The cloud-capped tow'rs, the gorgeous palaces,
> The solemn temples, the great globe itself,
> Yea, all which it inherit, shall dissolve,
> And, like this insubstantial pageant faded,
> Leave not a rack behind. We are such stuff
> As dreams are made on; and our little life
> Is rounded with a sleep.
> (IV.1.148–58)

When he speaks these words, Prospero has just presented a betrothal masque for Ferdinand and Miranda, and the spirit-actors, their revels having ended, immediately vanish. We watch Miranda and Ferdinand, unwitting actors in Prospero's plot, watch actors in a play-within-a-play. The distinction between art and life blurs further when we realize that the "great globe" refers to the literal theatre in which the actors played their parts. Life, like drama, is as evanescent as a dream, a passing show in the midst of oblivion. Although Prospero's statement recalls the weary detachment of Macbeth's vision of life as a "poor player" or Jaques's "all the world's a stage," it also suggests an awareness that life is more precious for its transience. Shakespeare is simultaneously preoccupied with his art and the reality that his art must depict. Several levels of theatricality operate within the play: *The Tempest* itself, Prospero's plot in which a deserted island suggests an empty stage (an analogy further strengthened by the fact that Shakespeare's theatre was without walls), and a wedding masque, all concluding with an epilogue in which the actor playing Prospero steps forth, revealing that he is only an ordinary man playing a part. With his words, the carefully constructed illusion dissolves.

Critics sometimes divide an artist's career into three phases, and the distinction, while simplistic, is helpful. In the first, his work is unselfconscious, exuberant; in the middle, he exhibits mature prowess and control; and, last stage of all, he is nostalgic, self-conscious, and so completely the master of his material that he playfully revives old themes and ideas in a new and intriguing way. Many of Shakespeare's works reveal an intense awareness of their own artifice, none more so than *The Tempest,* his last, most retrospective play. Shakespeare isn't simply rehashing old material; he is mixing themes together with such odd source materials as Montaigne's essay "On Cannibals," Ovid's *Metamorphoses,* travel literature, accounts of shipwrecks, and pamphlets about the New World—all creating a drama both nostalgic and innovative.

In both *King Lear* and *The Tempest* a storm marks the beginning of moral regeneration. The shipwreck itself looks back to both a comedy and a tragedy: *Twelfth Night,* in which another supposedly drowned character is restored to life; and *Macbeth,* in which another ship is magically "tempest-tossed." The marriage masque and the warring dukes recall *As You Like It;* and in its treatment of illusion and reality, *The Tempest* is a rewrite of *A Midsummer Night's Dream,* with Prospero taking the place of Oberon, and Ariel of Puck.

The Tempest opens with Prospero's plot to restore himself as the rightful Duke of Milan, to punish his brother and arrange a marriage between Miranda and

Ferdinand that will solidify the alliance between the two duchies. The sea storm, part of Prospero's plan to bring his evil brother Antonio to the island, also casts ashore the counsellor, Gonzalo; Alonso, Duke of Naples; his son Ferdinand; and the clowns Trinculo and Stephano. The ship is a microcosm of the world, with the castaways the group upon which Prospero practices his "art." Ariel, Prospero's stage manager, must keep a watchful eye on the crew, for when left on their own, Antonio and Sebastian plot to murder Gonzalo and Alonso, and Trinculo and Stephano join forces with Caliban to murder Prospero. An Elizabethan *Lord of the Flies*, *The Tempest* reveals that beyond civilization's constraining influence, human nature is a "thing of darkness." Still, despite these conspiracies and threats, we remain distanced from the dramatic action, secure in the knowledge that Prospero is in complete control and that no one is truly in danger.

But even playwrights and magicians have anxieties. Prospero worries endlessly that he won't be able to punish his brother, get his dukedom back, and cause Miranda and Ferdinand to fall in love within his allotted time span. Throughout the play we are reminded of the amount of time the men have been on the island. The shipwreck begins between two and three o'clock; at the end, when they all go in to dinner, it's about six o'clock. Not an arbitrary number: a performance at the Globe ran three hours, and Shakespeare's own power lasted for only that length of time. Mimetic and real time schemes coincide; the two plots, Prospero's and Shakespeare's, end at the same time. Just before his time runs out, Prospero suddenly realizes that he's left Stephano, Trinculo, and Caliban stuck in a swamp and must bring them back before the play ends.

It's easy to get caught up in the play's self-conscious artistry and forget its larger, more penetrating vision. *The Tempest* is more than magic and trickery. Prospero's spell works a change in the human heart, and *The Tempest* is ultimately about virtue, forgiveness, and love—human feelings, not godlike detachment. The transformations of art are entertaining, but metamorphosis within the self is more deeply satisfying. The "sea-sorrow" that the characters undergo ultimately leads to a "sea change." As soon as Alonso repents of his treachery, his son is immediately restored; the faithful Gonzalo embraces Prospero; Ariel is set free; Miranda and Ferdinand create a new alliance out of their fathers' enmity. Even the brutish Caliban says, "I'll be wise hereafter, / And seek for grace" (V.1.295–96). The play, which begins with disorder in the heavens, ends with a new order on earth.

Only Antonio remains unrepentant, and Prospero, who has scarcely been able to contain his rage throughout the play, abandons his revenge and forgives his brother, setting his own "nobler reason 'gainst [his] fury": "The rarer action is / In virtue than in vengeance' (V.1.26.27–28). As a civilized man, Prospero realizes that true civility—and civilization—depend on graciousness.

> For you, most wicked sir, whom to call brother
> Would even infect my mouth, I do forgive
> Thy rankest fault—all of them. . . .
> (V.1.130–32)

Antonio says nothing to this, his only other comment in the play being a nasty comment about Caliban. Thus we are reminded that although we may be transformed through suffering and love, some parts of human nature remain obdurate.

But to Miranda, who has known only her father, Caliban, and Ariel, humanity seems wondrous:

How many goodly creatures are there here!
How beauteous mankind is! O brave new world,
That has such people in't!
(V.1.183–85)

To which her father gently replies: "'Tis new to thee." Although Miranda is deluded, there is no bitterness in Prospero's remark. He tempers the joy of a first vision of the world with the compassionate understanding that each age must rediscover the world (and its evil) afresh.

In regaining his usurped dukedom in Milan, Prospero returns to Caliban the island he took from *him*. But before Prospero departs, he must claim his monster and free his sprite. Turning to Caliban, he says, "...this thing of darkness / I acknowledge mine" (V.1.275–76). Renouncing his godlike powers, Prospero must acknowledge himself as a man, and therefore he now can look upon Caliban, the uncivilized brute within us all, as a part of himself. His release of Ariel suggests that the imagination must remain unfettered, not chained to human desire.

Shakespeare ends *The Tempest* by asserting that human beings can't live solely in art—Prospero and Miranda belong in the ordinary world of time and mortality, where he will rule and she will marry and have children. Yet even as he endorses mortal life, the dramatist questions the nature of this "real" world. Prospero's plot concludes at six o'clock, with all the characters returning to his house for dinner, just at the time that Shakespeare's spectators would probably return from the Globe to *their* houses and sit down to *their* dinners. Illusion and reality merge as the actor playing Prospero steps forth with a plea to the audience:

> I must be here confined by you,
> Or sent to Naples. Let me not,
> Since I have my dukedom got
> And pardoned the deceiver, dwell
> In this bare island by your spell;
> But release me from my bands
> With the help of your good hands.
> (Epilogue, 4–10)

Just as Prospero set his spirit-actor, Ariel, free, we are asked to liberate this actor that he, too, may return home. Like the audience, like Prospero and Miranda, he will return to the real world, but he will only be exchanging one dream for another.

Related Readings

from A True Reportory of the Wreck and Redemption of Sir Thomas Gates, Knight

by William Strachey

Shakespeare lived during the Age of Exploration, when stories of voyages to new lands expanded people's knowledge of their world. Many scholars believe that Shakespeare was familiar with the following account of a hurricane and shipwreck off the coast of the Bermuda Islands in 1609. This vivid description could have easily provided inspiration for the setting of The Tempest.

[W]e were within seven or eight days at the most, by Captain Newport's reckoning, of making Cape Henry upon the coast of Virginia, when on ... July 24 ... the clouds gathering thick upon us and the winds singing and whistling most unusually (which made us to cast off our pinnace, towing the same until then astern), a dreadful storm and hideous began to blow from out the northeast, which, swelling and roaring as it were by fits, some hours with more violence than others, at length did beat all light from Heaven; which, like an hell of darkness, turned black upon us, so much the more fuller of horror as in such cases horror and fear use to overrun the troubled and overmastered senses of all, which taken up with amazement, the ears lay so sensible to the terrible cries and murmurs of the winds and distraction of our company as who was most armed and best prepared was not a little shaken. . . .

For four-and-twenty hours the storm in a restless tumult had blown so exceedingly as we could not apprehend in our imaginations any possibility of greater violence; yet did we still find it not only more terrible but more constant, fury added to fury, and one storm urging a second more outrageous than the former, whether it so wrought upon our fears or indeed met with new forces. Sometimes strikes [? shrieks] in our ship amongst women and passengers not used to such hurly and discomforts made us look one upon the other with troubled hearts and panting bosoms, our clamors drowned in the winds and the winds in thunder. Prayers might well be in the heart and lips but drowned in the outcries of the officers: nothing heard that could give comfort, nothing seen that might encourage hope. . . .

Our sails wound up lay without their use, and if at any time we bore but a hullock, or half forecourse, to guide her before the sea, six and sometimes eight men were not enough to hold the whipstaff in the steerage and the tiller below in the gunner room: by which may be imagined the strength of the storm, in which the sea swelled above the clouds and gave battle unto Heaven. It could not be said to rain: the waters like whole rivers did flood in the air. And this I did still observe: that whereas upon the land when a storm hath poured itself forth once in drifts of rain, the wind, as beaten down and vanquished therewith, not long after endureth; here the glut of water (as if throttling the wind erewhile) was no sooner a little emptied and qualified but instantly the winds (as having gotten their mouths now free and at liberty) spake more loud and grew more tumultuous and malignant. What shall I say? Winds and seas were as mad as fury and rage could make them. . . . [t]here was not a moment in which the sudden splitting of instant oversetting of the ship was not expected. . . .

Once so huge a sea brake upon the poop and quarter upon us as it covered our ship from stern to stem like a garment or a vast cloud; it filled her brim full for a while within, from the hatches up to the spardeck. The source or confluence of water was so violent as it rushed and carried the helm-man from the helm and wrested the whipstaff out of his hand, which so flew from side to side that when he would have seized the same again it so tossed him from starboard to larboard as it was God's mercy it had not split him. It so beat him from his hold and so bruised him as a fresh man hazarding in by chance fell fair with it and, by main strength bearing somewhat up, made good his place and with much clamor encouraged and called upon others, who gave her now up, rent in pieces and absolutely lost. . . .

During all this time the heavens looked so black upon us that it was not possible the elevation of the Pole might be observed; nor a star by night nor sunbeam by day was to be seen. Only upon the Thursday night Sir George Somers, being upon the watch, had an apparition of a little, round light, like a faint star, trembling and streaming along with a sparkling blaze, half the height upon the main mast and shooting sometimes from shroud to shroud, 'tempting to settle, as it were, upon any of the four shrouds. And for three or four hours together, or rather more, half the night, it kept with us, running sometimes along the main yard to the very end and then returning; at which Sir George Somers called divers about him and showed them the same, who observed it with much wonder and carefulness. But upon a sudden, toward the morning watch, they lost the sight of it and knew not what way it made. . . .

And it being now Friday, the fourth morning, it wanted little but that there had been a general determination to have shut up hatches and, commending our sinful souls to God, committed the ship to the mercy of the gale. Surely, that night we must have done it, and that night had we then perished. But see the goodness and sweet introduction of better hope by our merciful God given unto us: Sir George Somers, when no man dreamed of such happiness, had discovered and cried land. . . .

[w]e had got her [the ship] within a mile under the southeast point of the land, where we had somewhat smooth water. But having no hope to save her by coming to an anchor in the same, we were enforced to run her ashore as near the land as we could, which brought us within three quarters of a mile of shore; and by the mercy of God unto us, making out our boats, we had ere night brought all our men, women, and children, about the number of 150, safe into the island.

We found it to be the dangerous and dreaded island, or rather islands, of the Bermuda; whereof let me give Your Ladyship a brief description before I proceed to my narration. And that the rather because they be so terrible to all that ever touched on them, and such tempests, thunders, and other fearful objects are seen and heard about them, that they be called commonly the Devil's Islands and are feared and avoided of all sea travelers alive above any other place in the world. Yet it pleased our merciful God to make even this hideous and hated place both the place of our safety and means of our deliverance.

And hereby, also, I hope to deliver the world from a foul and general error, it being counted of most that they can be no habitation for men but rather given over to devils and wicked spirits; whereas indeed we find them now by experience to be as habitable and commodious as most countries of the same climate and situation, insomuch as, if the entrance into them were as easy as the place itself is contenting, it had long ere this been inhabited as well as other islands.

Related Readings

The Sire de Malétroit's Door

by Robert Louis Stevenson

With the help of the spirit Ariel, Prospero craftily sets up the romance between Miranda and Ferdinand. In this story, an old uncle works a little magic of his own to bring together his niece and a bewildered young man.

Denis de Beaulieu was not yet two-and-twenty, but he counted himself a grown man, and a very accomplished cavalier into the bargain. Lads were early formed in that rough, warfaring epoch; and when one has been in a pitched battle and a dozen raids, has killed one's man in an honourable fashion, and knows a thing or two of strategy and mankind, a certain swagger in the gait is surely to be pardoned. He had put up his horse with due care, and supped with due deliberation; and then, in a very agreeable frame of mind, went out to pay a visit in the grey of the evening. It was not a very wise proceeding on the young man's part. He would have done better to remain beside the fire or go decently to bed. For the town was full of the troops of Burgundy and England under a mixed command; and though Denis was there on safe-conduct, his safe-conduct was like to serve him little on a chance encounter.

It was September, 1429; the weather had fallen sharp; a flighty piping wind, laden with showers, beat about the township; and the dead leaves ran riot along the streets. Here and there a window was already lighted up; and the noise of men-at-arms making merry over supper within, came forth in fits and was swallowed up and carried away by the wind. The night fell swiftly; the flag of England, fluttering on the spire-top, grew ever fainter and fainter against the flying clouds—a black speck like a swallow in the tumultuous, leaden chaos of the sky. As the night fell the wind rose and began to hoot under archways and roar amid the treetops in the valley below the town.

Denis de Beaulieu walked fast and was soon knocking at his friend's door; but though he promised himself to stay only a little while and make an early return, his welcome was so pleasant, and he found so much to delay him, that it was already long past midnight before he said good-bye upon the threshold. The wind had fallen again in the meanwhile; the night was as black as the grave; not a star, nor a glimmer of moonshine, slipped through the canopy of cloud. Denis was ill-acquainted with the intricate lanes of Chateau Landon; even by daylight he had found some trouble in picking his way; and in this absolute darkness he soon lost it altogether. He was certain of one thing only—to keep mounting the hill; for his friend's house lay at the lower end, or tail, of Chateau Landon, while the inn was up at the head, under the great church spire. With this clue to go upon he stumbled and groped forward, now breathing more freely in open places where there was a good slice of sky overhead, now feeling along the wall in stifling closes. It is an eerie and mysterious position to be thus submerged in opaque blackness in an almost unknown town. The silence is terrifying in its possibilities. The touch of cold window bars to the exploring hand startles the man like the touch of a toad; the inequalities of the pavement shake his heart into his mouth; a piece of denser darkness threatens an ambuscade or a chasm in the pathway; and where the air is brighter, the houses put on strange and bewildering appearances, as if to lead him farther from his way. For Denis, who had to regain his inn without attracting notice, there was real danger as well as mere discomfort in the walk; and he went warily and boldly at once, and at every corner paused to make an observation.

He had been for some time threading a lane so narrow that he could touch a wall with either hand, when it began to open out and go sharply downward. Plainly this lay no longer in the direction of his inn; but the hope of a little more light tempted him forward to reconnoitre. The lane ended in a terrace with a bartisan wall, which gave an outlook between high houses, as out of an embrasure, into the valley lying dark and formless several hundred feet below. Denis looked down, and could discern a few tree-tops waving and a single speck of brightness where the river ran across a weir. The weather was clearing up, and the sky had lightened, so as to show the outline of the heavier clouds and the dark margin of the hills. By the uncertain glimmer, the house on his left hand should be a place of some pretensions; it was surmounted by several pinnacles and turret-tops; the round stern of a chapel, with a fringe of flying buttresses, projected boldly from the main block; and the door was sheltered under a deep porch carved with figures and overhung by two long gargoyles. The windows of the chapel gleamed through their intricate tracery with a light as of many tapers, and threw out the buttresses and the peaked roof in a more intense blackness against the sky. It was plainly the hotel of some great family of the neighbourhood; and as it reminded Denis of a town house of his own at Bourges, he stood for some time gazing up at it and mentally gauging the skill of the architects and the consideration of the two families.

There seemed to be no issue to the terrace but the lane by which he had reached it; he could only retrace his steps, but he had gained some notion of his whereabouts, and hoped by this means to hit the main thoroughfare and speedily regain the inn. He was reckoning without that chapter of accidents which was to make this night memorable above all others in his career; for he had not gone back above a hundred yards before he saw a light coming to meet him, and heard loud voices speaking together in the echoing of the lane. It was a party of men-at-arms going the night round with torches. Denis assured himself that they had all been making free with the wine-bowl, and were in no mood to be particular about safe-conducts or the niceties of chivalrous war. It was as like as not that they would kill him like a dog and leave him where he fell. The situation was inspiriting but nervous. Their own torches would conceal him from sight, he reflected; and he hoped that they would drown the noise of his footsteps with their own empty voices. If he were but fleet and silent, he might evade their notice altogether.

Unfortunately, as he turned to beat a retreat, his foot rolled upon a pebble; he fell against the wall with an ejaculation, and his sword rang loudly on the stones. Two or three voices demanded who went there—some in French, some in English; but Denis made no reply, and ran the faster down the lane. Once upon the terrace, he paused to look back. They still kept calling after him, and just then began to double the pace in pursuit, with a considerable clank of armour, and great tossing of the torchlight to and fro in the narrow jaws of the passage.

Denis cast a look around and darted into the porch. There he might escape observation, or—if that were too much to expect—was in a capital posture whether for parley or defence. So thinking, he drew his sword and tried to set his back against the door. To his surprise, it yielded behind his weight; and though he turned in a moment, continued to swing back on oiled and noiseless hinges, until it stood wide open on a black interior. When things fall out opportunely for the person concerned, he is not apt to be critical about the how or why, his own immediate personal convenience seeming a sufficient reason for the strangest oddities and revolutions in our sublunary things; and so Denis, without a moment's hesitation, stepped within and partly closed the door behind him to conceal his place of refuge. Nothing was further from his thoughts than to close it altogether; but for some inexplicable reason—perhaps by a spring or a weight—the ponderous mass of oak whipped itself out of his fingers and clanked to, with a formidable rumble and a noise like the falling of an automatic bar.

The round, at that very moment, debouched upon the terrace and proceeded to summon him with shouts and curses. He heard them ferreting in the dark corners; and the stock of a lance even rattled along the outer surface of the door behind which he stood; but these gentlemen were in too high a humour to be long delayed, and soon made off down a corkscrew pathway which had escaped Denis's observation, and passed out of sight and hearing along the battlements of the town.

Denis breathed again. He gave them a few minutes' grace for fear of accidents, and then groped about for some means of opening the door and slipping forth again. The inner surface was quite smooth, not a handle, not a moulding, not a projection of any sort. He got his finger-nails round the edges and pulled, but the mass was immovable. He shook it, it was as firm as a rock. Denis de Beaulieu frowned and gave vent to a little noiseless whistle. What ailed the door? he wondered. Why was it open? How came it to shut so easily and so effectually after him? There was something obscure and underhand about all this, that was little to the young man's fancy. It looked like a snare; and yet who would suppose a snare in such a quiet by-street and in a house of so prosperous and even noble an exterior? And yet—snare or no snare, intentionally or unintentionally—here he was, prettily trapped; and for the life of him he could see no way out of it again. The darkness began to weigh upon him. He gave ear; all was silent without, but within and close by he seemed to catch a faint sighing, a faint sobbing rustle, a little stealthy creak—as though many persons were at his side, holding themselves quite still, and governing even their respiration with the extreme of slyness. The idea went to his vitals with a shock, and he faced about suddenly as if to defend his life. Then, for the first time, he became aware of a light about the level of his eyes and at some distance in the interior of the house—a vertical thread of light, widening towards the bottom, such as might escape between two wings of arras over a doorway. To see anything was a relief to Denis; it was like a piece of solid ground to a man labouring in a morass; his mind seized upon it with avidity; and he stood staring at it and trying to piece together some logical conception of his surroundings. Plainly there was a flight of steps ascending from his own level to that of this illuminated doorway; and indeed he thought he could make out another thread of light, as fine as a needle and as faint as phosphorescence, which might very well be reflected along the polished wood of a handrail. Since he had begun to suspect that he was not alone, his heart had continued to beat with smothering violence, and an intolerable desire for action of any sort had possessed itself of his spirit. He was in deadly peril, he believed. What could be more natural than to mount the staircase, lift the curtain, and confront his difficulty at once? At least he would be dealing with something tangible; at least he would be no longer in the dark. He stepped slowly forward with outstretched hands, until his foot struck the bottom step; then he rapidly scaled the stairs, stood for a moment to compose his expression, lifted the arras and went in.

He found himself in a large apartment of polished stone. There were three doors; one on each of three sides; all similarly curtained with tapestry. The fourth side was occupied by two large windows and a great stone chimney-piece, carved with the arms of the Malétroits. Denis recognised the bearings, and was gratified to find himself in such good hands. The room was strongly illuminated; but it contained little furniture except a heavy table and a chair or two, the hearth was innocent of fire, and the pavement was but sparsely strewn with rushes clearly many days old.

On a high chair beside the chimney, and directly facing Denis as he entered, sat a little old gentleman in a fur tippet. He sat with his legs crossed and his hands folded, and a cup of spiced wine stood by his elbow on a bracket on the wall. His countenance had a strongly masculine cast; not properly human, but such as we see in the bull, the goat, or the domestic boar; something equivocal and wheedling, something greedy, brutal, and dangerous. The upper lip was inordinately full, as though swollen by a blow or a toothache; and the smile, the peaked eyebrows, and the small, strong eyes were quaintly and almost comically evil in expression. Beautiful white hair hung straight all round his head, like a saint's, and fell in a single curl upon the tippet. His beard and moustache were the pink of venerable sweetness. Age, probably in consequence of inordinate precautions, had left no mark upon his hands; and the Malétroit hand was famous. It would be difficult to imagine anything at once so fleshy and so delicate in design; the taper, sensual fingers were like those of one of Leonardo's women; the fork of the thumb made a dimpled protuberance when closed; the nails were perfectly shaped, and of a dead, surprising whiteness. It rendered his aspect tenfold more redoubtable, that a man with hands like these should keep them devoutly folded in his lap like a virgin martyr—that a man with so intense and startling an expression of face should sit patiently on his seat and contemplate people with an unwinking stare, like a god, or a god's statue. His quiescence seemed ironical and treacherous, it fitted so poorly with his looks.

Such was Alain, Sire de Malétroit.

Denis and he looked silently at each other for a second or two.

"Pray step in," said the Sire de Malétroit. "I have been expecting you all the evening."

He had not risen, but he accompanied his words with a smile and a slight but courteous inclination of the head. Partly from the smile, partly from the strange musical murmur with which the Sire prefaced his observation, Denis felt a strong shudder of disgust go through his marrow. And what with disgust and honest confusion of mind, he could scarcely get words together in reply.

"I fear," he said, "that this is a double accident. I am not the person you suppose me. It seems you were looking for a visit; but for my part, nothing was further from my thoughts—nothing could be more contrary to my wishes—than this intrusion."

"Well, well," replied the old gentleman indulgently, "here you are, which is the main point. Seat yourself, my friend, and put yourself entirely at your ease. We shall arrange our little affairs presently."

Denis perceived that the matter was still complicated with some misconception, and he hastened to continue his explanations.

"Your door . . ." he began.

"About my door?" asked the other, raising his peaked eyebrows. "A little piece of ingenuity." And he shrugged his shoulders. "A hospitable fancy! By your own account, you were not desirous of making my acquaintance. We old people look for such reluctance now and then; and when it touches our honour, we cast about until we find some way of overcoming it. You arrive uninvited, but believe me, very welcome."

"You persist in error, sir," said Denis. "There can be no question between you and me. I am a stranger in this countryside. My name is Denis, damoiseau de Beaulieu. If you see me in your house, it is only—"

"My young friend," interrupted the other, "you will permit me to have my own ideas on that subject. They probably differ from yours at the present moment," he added with a leer, "but time will show which of us is in the right."

Denis was convinced he had to do with a lunatic. He seated himself with a shrug, content to wait the upshot; and a pause ensued, during which he thought he could distinguish a hurried gabbling as of prayer from behind the arras immediately opposite him. Sometimes there seemed to be but one person engaged, sometimes two; and the vehemence of the voice, low as it was, seemed to indicate either great haste or an agony of spirit. It occurred to him that this piece of tapestry covered the entrance to the chapel he had noticed from without.

The old gentleman meanwhile surveyed Denis from head to foot with a smile, and from time to time emitted little noises like a bird or a mouse, which seemed to indicate a high degree of satisfaction. This state of matters became rapidly insupportable; and Denis, to put an end to it, remarked politely that the wind had gone down.

The old gentleman fell into a fit of silent laughter, so prolonged and violent that he became quite red in the face. Denis got upon his feet at once, and put on his hat with a flourish.

"Sir," he said, "if you are in your wits, you have affronted me grossly. If you are out of them, I flatter myself I can find better employment for my brains than to talk with lunatics. My conscience is clear; you have made a fool of me from the first moment; you have refused to hear my explanations; and now there is no power under God will make me stay here any longer; and if I cannot make my way out in a more decent fashion, I will hack your door in pieces with my sword."

The Sire de Malétroit raised his right hand and wagged it at Denis with the fore and little fingers extended.

"My dear nephew," he said, "sit down."

"Nephew!" retorted Denis, "you lie in your throat;" and he snapped his fingers in his face.

"Sit down, you rogue!" cried the old gentleman, in a sudden harsh voice, like the barking of a dog. "Do you fancy," he went on, "that when I had made my little contrivance for the door I had stopped short with that? If you prefer to be bound hand and foot till your bones ache, rise and try to go away. If you choose to remain a free young buck, agreeably conversing with an old gentleman—why, sit where you are in peace, and God be with you."

"Do you mean I am a prisoner?" demanded Denis.

"I state the facts," replied the other. "I would rather leave the conclusion to yourself."

Denis sat down again. Externally he managed to keep pretty calm; but within, he was now boiling with anger, now chilled with apprehension. He no longer felt convinced that he was dealing with a madman. And if the old gentleman was sane, what, in God's name, had he to look for? What absurd or tragical adventure had befallen him? What countenance was he to assume?

While he was thus unpleasantly reflecting, the arras

that overhung the chapel door was raised, and a tall priest in his robes came forth and, giving a long, keen stare at Denis, said something in an undertone to Sire de Malétroit.

"She is in a better frame of spirit?" asked the latter.

"She is more resigned, messire," replied the priest.

"Now the Lord help her, she is hard to please!" sneered the old gentleman. "A likely stripling—not ill-born—and of her own choosing, too? Why, what more would the jade have?"

"The situation is not usual for a young damsel," said the other, "and somewhat trying to her blushes."

"She should have thought of that before she began the dance. It was none of my choosing, God knows that: but since she is in it, by our Lady, she shall carry it to the end." And then addressing Denis, "Monsieur de Beaulieu," he asked, "may I present you to my niece? She has been waiting your arrival, I may say, with even greater impatience than myself."

Denis had resigned himself with a good grace—all he desired was to know the worst of it as speedily as possible; so he rose at once, and bowed in acquiescence. The Sire de Malétroit followed his example and limped, with the assistance of the chaplain's arm, towards the chapel door. The priest pulled aside the arras, and all three entered. The building had considerable architectural pretensions. A light groining sprang from six stout columns, and hung down in two rich pendants from the centre of the vault. The place terminated behind the altar in a round end, embossed and honeycombed with a superfluity of ornament in relief, and pierced by many little windows shaped like stars, trefoils, or wheels. These windows were imperfectly glazed, so that the night air circulated freely in the chapel. The tapers, of which there must have been half a hundred burning on the altar, were unmercifully blown about; and the light went through many different phases of brilliancy and semi-eclipse. On the steps in front of the altar knelt a young girl richly attired as a bride. A chill settled over Denis as he observed her costume; he fought with desperate energy against the conclusion that was thrust upon his mind; it could not—it should not—be as he feared.

"Blanche," said the Sire, in his most flute-like tones, "I have brought a friend to see you, my little girl; turn round and give him your pretty hand. It is good to be devout; but it is necessary to be polite, my niece."

The girl rose to her feet and turned towards the new comers. She moved all of a piece; and shame and exhaustion were expressed in every line of her fresh young body; and she held her head down and kept her eyes upon the pavement, as she came slowly forward. In the course of her advance, her eyes fell upon Denis de Beaulieu's feet—feet of which he was justly vain, be it remarked, and wore in the most elegant accoutrement even while travelling. She paused—started, as if his yellow boots had conveyed some shocking meaning—and glanced suddenly up into the wearer's countenance. Their eyes met; shame gave place to horror and terror in her looks; the blood left her lips; with a piercing scream she covered her face with her hands and sank upon the chapel floor.

"That is not the man!" she cried. "My uncle, that is not the man!"

The Sire de Malétroit chirped agreeably. "Of course not," he said; "I expected as much. It was so unfortunate you could not remember his name."

"Indeed," she cried, "indeed, I have never seen this person till this moment—I have never so much as set eyes upon him—I never wish to see him again. Sir," she said, turning to Denis, "if you are a gentleman, you will bear me out. Have I ever seen you—have you ever seen me—before this accursed hour?"

"To speak for myself, I have never had that pleasure," answered the young man. "This is the first time, messire, that I have met with your engaging niece."

The old gentleman shrugged his shoulders.

"I am distressed to hear it," he said. "But it is never too late to begin. I had little more acquaintance with my own late lady ere I married her; which proves," he added with a grimace, "that these impromptu marriages may often produce an excellent understanding in the long run. As the bridegroom is to have a voice in the matter, I will give him two hours to make up for lost time before we proceed with the ceremony." And he turned towards the door, followed by the clergyman.

The girl was on her feet in a moment. "My uncle, you cannot be in earnest," she said. "I declare before God I will stab myself rather than be forced on that young man. The heart rises at it; God forbid such marriages; you dishonour your white hair. Oh, my uncle, pity me! There is not a woman in all the world but would prefer death to such a nuptial. Is it possible," she added, faltering, "is it possible that you do not believe me—that you still think this"—and she pointed at Denis with a tremor of anger and contempt—"that you still think *this* to be the man?"

"Frankly," said the old gentleman, pausing on the threshold, "I do. But let me explain to you once for all, Blanche de Malétroit, my way of thinking about this affair. When you took it into your head to dishonour my family and the name that I have borne, in peace and war, for more than three-score years, you forfeited, not only the right to question my designs, but that of looking me in the face. If your father had been alive, he would have spat on you and turned you out of doors. His was the hand of iron. You may bless your God you have only to deal with the hand of velvet, mademoiselle. It was my duty to get you married without delay. Out of pure goodwill, I have tried to find your own gallant for you. And I believe I have succeeded. But before God and all the holy angels, Blanche de Malétroit, if I have not, I care not one jackstraw. So let me recommend you to be polite to our young friend; for upon my word, your next groom may be less appetising."

And with that he went out, with the chaplain at his heels; and the arras fell behind the pair.

The girl turned upon Denis with flashing eyes.

"And what, sir," she demanded, "may be the meaning of all this?"

"God knows," returned Denis gloomily. "I am a prisoner in this house, which seems full of mad people. More I know not; and nothing do I understand."

"And pray how came you here?" she asked.

He told her as briefly as he could. "For the rest," he added, "perhaps you will follow my example, and tell me the answer to all these riddles, and what, in God's name, is like to be the end of it."

She stood silent for a little, and he could see her lips tremble and her tearless eyes burn with a feverish lustre. Then she pressed her forehead in both hands.

"Alas, how my head aches!" she said wearily—"to say nothing of my poor heart! But it is due to you to know my story, unmaidenly as it must seem. I am called Blanche de Malétroit; I have been without father or mother for—oh! for as long as I can recollect, and indeed I have been most unhappy all my life. Three months ago a young captain began to stand near me every day in church. I could see that I pleased him; I am much to blame, but I was so glad that anyone should love me; and when he passed me a letter, I took it home with me and read it with great pleasure. Since that time he has written many. He was so anxious to speak with me, poor fellow! and kept asking me to leave the door open some evening that we might have two words upon the stair. For he knew how much my uncle trusted me." She gave something like a sob at that, and it was a moment before she could go on. "My uncle is a hard man, but he is very shrewd," she said at last. "He has performed many feats in war, and was a great person at court, and much trusted by Queen Isabeau in old days. How he came to suspect me I cannot tell; but it is hard to keep anything from his knowledge; and this morning, as we came from mass, he took my hand in his, forced it open, and read my little billet, walking by my side all the while. When he had finished, he gave it back to me with great politeness. It contained another request to have the door left open; and this has been the ruin of us all. My uncle kept me strictly in my room until evening, and then ordered me to dress myself as you see me—a hard mockery for a young girl, do you not think so? I suppose, when he could not prevail with me to tell him the young captain's name, he must have laid a trap for him: into which, alas! you have fallen in the anger of God. I looked for much confusion; for how could I tell whether he was willing to take me for his wife on these sharp terms? He might have been trifling with me from the first; or I might have made myself too cheap in his eyes. But truly I had not looked for such a shameful punishment as this! I could not think that God would let a girl be so disgraced before a young man. And now I have told you all; and I can scarcely hope that you will not despise me."

Denis made her a respectful inclination.

"Madam," he said, "you have honoured me by your confidence. It remains for me to prove that I am not unworthy of the honour. Is Messire de Malétroit at hand?"

"I believe he is writing in the salle without," she answered.

"May I lead you thither, madam?" asked Denis, offering his hand with his most courtly bearing.

She accepted it; and the pair passed out of the chapel, Blanche in a very drooping and shamefast condition, but Denis strutting and ruffling in the consciousness of a mission, and the boyish certainty of accomplishing it with honour.

The Sire de Malétroit rose to meet them with an ironical obeisance.

"Sir," said Denis with the grandest possible air, "I believe I am to have some say in the matter of this marriage; and let me tell you at once, I will be no party to forcing the inclination of this young lady. Had it been freely offered to me, I should have been proud to accept her hand, for I perceive she is as good as she is beautiful; but as things are, I have now the honour, messire, of refusing."

Blanche looked at him with gratitude in her eyes; but the old gentleman only smiled and smiled, until his smile grew positively sickening to Denis.

"I am afraid," he said, "Monsieur de Beaulieu, that you do not perfectly understand the choice I have to offer you. Follow me, I beseech you, to this window." And he led the way to one of the large windows which stood open on the night. "You observe," he went on, "there is an iron ring in the upper masonry, and reeved through that, a very efficacious rope. Now, mark my words; if you should find your disinclination to my niece's person insurmountable, I shall have you hanged out of this window before sunrise. I shall only proceed to such an extremity with the greatest regret, you may believe me. For it is not at all your death that I desire, but my niece's establishment in life. At the same time, it must come to that if you prove obstinate. Your family, Monsieur de Beaulieu, is very well in its way; but if you sprang from Charlemagne, you should not refuse the hand of a Malétroit with impunity—not if she had been as common as the Paris road—not if she were as hideous as the gargoyle over my door. Neither my niece nor you, nor my own private feelings, move me at all in this matter. The honour of my house has been compromised; I believe you to be the guilty person; at least you are now in the secret; and you can hardly wonder if I request you to wipe out the stain. If you will not, your blood be on your own head! It will be no great satisfaction to me to have your interesting relics kicking their heels in the breeze below my windows; but half a loaf is better than no bread, and if I cannot cure the dishonour, I shall at least stop the scandal."

There was a pause.

"I believe there are other ways of settling such imbroglios among gentlemen," said Denis. "You wear a sword, and I hear you have used it with distinction."

The Sire de Malétroit made a signal to the chaplain, who crossed the room with long silent strides and raised the arras over the third of the three doors. It was only a moment before he let it fall again; but Denis had time to see a dusky passage full of armed men.

"When I was a little younger, I should have been delighted to honour you, Monsieur de Beaulieu," said Sire Alain; "but I am now too old. Faithful retainers are the sinews of age, and I must employ the strength I have. This is one of the hardest things to swallow as a man grows up in years; but with a little patience, even this becomes habitual. You and the lady seem to prefer the salle for what remains of your two hours; and as I have no desire to cross your preference, I shall resign it to your use with all the pleasure in the world. No haste!" he added, holding up his hand, as he saw a dangerous look come into Denis de Beaulieu's face. "If your mind revolts against hanging, it will be time enough two hours hence to throw yourself out of the window or upon the pikes of my retainers. Two hours of life are always two hours. A great many things may turn up in even as little a while as that. And, besides, if I understand her appearance, my niece has still something to say to you. You will not disfigure your last hours by a want of politeness to a lady?"

Denis looked at Blanche, and she made him an imploring gesture.

It is likely that the old gentleman was hugely pleased at this symptom of an understanding; for he smiled on both, and added sweetly: "If you will give me your word of honour, Monsieur de Beaulieu, to wait my return at the end of the two hours before attempting anything desperate, I shall withdraw my retainers, and let you speak in greater privacy with mademoiselle."

Denis again glanced at the girl, who seemed to beseech him to agree.

"I give you my word of honour," he said.

Messire de Malétroit bowed, and proceeded to limp about the apartment, clearing his throat the while with that odd musical chirp which had already grown so irritating in the ears of Denis de Beaulieu. He first possessed himself of some papers which lay upon the table; then he went to the mouth of the passage and appeared to give an order to the men behind the arras; and lastly he hobbled out through the door by which Denis had come in, turning upon the threshold to address a last smiling bow to the young couple, and followed by the chaplain with a hand-lamp.

No sooner were they alone than Blanche advanced towards Denis with her hands extended. Her face was flushed and excited, and her eyes shone with tears.

"You shall not die!" she cried, "you shall marry me after all."

"You seem to think, madam," replied Denis, "that I stand much in fear of death."

"Oh no, no," she said, "I see you are no poltroon.

It is for my own sake—I could not bear to have you slain for such a scruple."

"I am afraid," returned Denis, "that you underrate the difficulty, madam. What you may be too generous to refuse, I may be too proud to accept. In a moment of noble feeling towards me, you forgot what you perhaps owe to others."

He had the decency to keep his eyes upon the floor as he said this, and after he had finished, so as not to spy upon her confusion. She stood silent for a moment, then walked suddenly away, and falling on her uncle's chair, fairly burst out sobbing. Denis was in the acme of embarrassment. He looked round, as if to seek for inspiration, and seeing a stool, plumped down upon it for something to do. There he sat, playing with the guard of his rapier, and wishing himself dead a thousand times over, and buried in the nastiest kitchen-heap in France. His eyes wandered round the apartment, but found nothing to arrest them. There were such wide spaces between the furniture, the light fell so badly and cheerlessly over all, the dark outside air looked in so coldly through the windows, that he thought he had never seen a church so vast, nor a tomb so melancholy. The regular sobs of Blanche de Malétroit measured out the time like the ticking of a clock. He read the device upon the shield over and over again, until his eyes became obscured; he stared into shadowy corners until he imagined they were swarming with horrible animals; and every now and again he awoke with a start, to remember that his last two hours were running, and death was on the march.

Oftener and oftener, as the time went on, did his glance settle on the girl herself. Her face was bowed forward and covered with her hands, and she was shaken at intervals by the convulsive hiccup of grief. Even thus she was not an unpleasant object to dwell upon, so plump and yet so fine, with a warm brown skin, and the most beautiful hair, Denis thought, in the whole world of womankind. Her hands were like her uncle's; but they were more in place at the end of her young arms, and looked infinitely soft and caressing. He remembered how her blue eyes had shone upon him, full of anger, pity, and innocence. And the more he dwelt on her perfections, the uglier death looked, and the more deeply was he smitten with penitence at her continued tears. Now he felt that no man could have the courage to leave a world which contained so beautiful a creature; and now he would have given forty minutes of his last hour to have unsaid his cruel speech.

Suddenly a hoarse and ragged peal of cockcrow rose to their ears from the dark valley below the windows. And this shattering noise in the silence of all around was like a light in a dark place, and shook them both out of their reflections.

"Alas, can I do nothing to help you?" she said, looking up.

"Madam," replied Denis, with a fine irrelevancy, "if I have said anything to wound you, believe me, it was for your own sake and not for mine."

She thanked him with a tearful look.

"I feel your position cruelly," he went on. "The world has been bitter hard on you. Your uncle is a disgrace to mankind. Believe me, madam, there is no young gentleman in all France but would be glad of my opportunity to die in doing you a momentary service."

"I know already that you can be very brave and generous," she answered. "What I *want* to know is whether I can serve you—now or afterwards," she added, with a quaver.

"Most certainly," he answered with a smile. "Let me sit beside you as if I were a friend, instead of a foolish intruder; try to forget how awkwardly we are placed to one another; make my last moments go pleasantly; and you will do me the chief service possible."

"You are very gallant," she added, with a yet deeper sadness . . . "very gallant . . . and it somehow pains me. But draw nearer, if you please; and if you find anything to say to me, you will at least make certain of a very friendly listener. Ah! Monsieur de Beaulieu," she broke forth—"ah! Monsieur de Beaulieu, how can I look you in the face?" And she fell to weeping again with a renewed effusion.

"Madam," said Denis, taking her hand in both of his, "reflect on the little time I have before me, and the great bitterness into which I am cast by the sight of your distress. Spare me, in my last moments, the spectacle of what I cannot cure even with the sacrifice of my life."

"I am very selfish," answered Blanche. "I will be braver, Monsieur de Beaulieu, for your sake. But think if I can do you no kindness in the future—if you have no friends to whom I could carry your adieux. Charge me as heavily as you can; every burden will lighten, by so little, the invaluable gratitude I owe you. Put it in my power to do something more for you than weep."

"My mother is married again, and has a young family to care for. My brother Guichard will inherit my fiefs; and if I am not in error, that will content him amply for my death. Life is a little vapour that passeth away, as we are told by those in holy orders. When a man is in a fair way and sees all life open in front of him, he seems to himself to make a very important figure in the world. His horse whinnies to him; the trumpets blow and the girls look out of window as he rides into town before his company; he receives many assurances of trust and regard—sometimes by express in a letter—sometimes face to face, with persons of great consequence falling on his neck. It is not wonderful if his head is turned for a time. But once he is dead, were he as brave as Hercules or as wise as Solomon, he is soon forgotten. It is not ten years since my father fell, with many other knights around him, in a very fierce encounter, and I do not think that any one of them, nor so much as the name of the fight, is now remembered. No, no, madam, the nearer you come to it, you see that death is a dark and dusty corner, where a man gets into his tomb and has the door shut after him till the judgment day. I have few friends just now, and once I am dead I shall have none."

"Ah, Monsieur de Beaulieu!" she exclaimed, "you forget Blanche de Malétroit."

"You have a sweet nature, madam, and you are pleased to estimate a little service far beyond its worth."

"It is not that," she answered. "You mistake me if you think I am so easily touched by my own concerns. I say so, because you are the noblest man I have ever met; because I recognise in you a spirit that would have made even a common person famous in the land."

"And yet here I die in a mouse-trap—with no more noise about it than my own squeaking," answered he.

A look of pain crossed her face, and she was silent for a little while. Then a light came into her eyes, and with a smile she spoke again.

"I cannot have my champion think meanly of himself. Anyone who gives his life for another will be met in Paradise by all the heralds and angels of the Lord God. And you have no such cause to hang your head. For . . . Pray, do you think me beautiful?" she asked, with a deep flush.

"Indeed, madam, I do," he said.

"I am glad of that," she answered heartily. "Do you think there are many men in France who have been asked in marriage by a beautiful maiden—with her own lips—and who have refused her to her face? I know you men would half despise such a triumph; but believe me, we women know more of what is precious in love. There is nothing that should set a person higher in his own esteem; and we women would prize nothing more dearly."

"You are very good," he said; "but you cannot make me forget that I was asked in pity and not for love."

"I am not so sure of that," she replied, holding down her head. "Hear me to an end, Monsieur de Beaulieu. I know how you must despise me; I feel you are right to do so; I am too poor a creature to occupy one thought of your mind, although, alas! you must die for me this morning. But when I asked you to marry me, indeed, and indeed, it was because I respected and admired you, and loved you with my whole soul, from the very moment that you took my part against my uncle. If you had seen yourself, and how noble you looked, you would pity rather than despise me. And now," she went on, hurriedly checking him with her hand, "although I have laid aside all reserve and told you so much, remember that I know your sentiments towards me already. I would not, believe me, being nobly born, weary you with importunities into consent. I too have a pride of my own: and I declare before the holy mother of God, if you should now go back from your word already given, I would no more marry you than I would marry my uncle's groom."

Denis smiled a little bitterly.

"It is a small love," he said, "that shies at a little pride."

She made no answer, although she probably had her own thoughts.

"Come hither to the window," he said, with a sigh. "Here is the dawn."

And indeed the dawn was already beginning. The

hollow of the sky was full of essential daylight, colourless and clean; and the valley underneath was flooded with a grey reflection. A few thin vapours clung in the coves of the forest or lay along the winding course of the river. The scene disengaged a surprising effect of stillness, which was hardly interrupted when the cocks began once more to crow among the steadings. Perhaps the same fellow who had made so horrid a clangour in the darkness not half-an-hour before, now sent up the merriest cheer to greet the coming day. A little wind went bustling and eddying among the tree-tops underneath the windows. And still the daylight kept flooding insensibly out of the east, which was soon to grow incandescent and cast up that red-hot cannon-ball, the rising sun.

Denis looked out over all this with a bit of a shiver. He had taken her hand, and retained it in his almost unconsciously.

"Has the day begun already?" she said; and then, illogically enough: "the night has been so long! Alas! what shall we say to my uncle when he returns?"

"What you will," said Denis, and he pressed her fingers in his.

She was silent.

"Blanche," he said, with a swift, uncertain, passionate utterance, "you have seen whether I fear death. You must know well enough that I would as gladly leap out of that window into the empty air as lay a finger on you without your free and full consent. But if you care for me at all do not let me lose my life in a misapprehension; for I love you better than the whole world; and though I will die for you blithely, it would be like all the joys of Paradise to live on and spend my life in your service."

As he stopped speaking, a bell began to ring loudly in the interior of the house; and a clatter of armour in the corridor showed that the retainers were returning to their post, and the two hours were at an end.

"After all that you have heard?" she whispered, leaning towards him with her lips and eyes.

"I have heard nothing," he replied.

"The captain's name was Florimond de Champdivers," she said in his ear.

"I did not hear it," he answered, taking her supple body in his arms and covering her wet face with kisses.

A melodious chirping was audible behind, followed by a beautiful chuckle, and the voice of Messire de Malétroit wished his new nephew a good morning.

Related Readings

Rappaccini's Daughter

by Nathaniel Hawthorne

This famous 19th-century story about a young woman, her father, and an eligible young man may remind you of Miranda, Prospero, and Ferdinand in The Tempest. *The ending, however, is where the similarity ends.*

A young man, named Giovanni Guasconti, came, very long ago, from the more southern region of Italy, to pursue his studies at the University of Padua. Giovanni, who had but a scanty supply of gold ducats in his pocket, took lodgings in a high and gloomy chamber of an old edifice which looked not unworthy to have been the palace of a Paduan noble, and which, in fact, exhibited over its entrance the armorial bearings of a family long since extinct. The young stranger, who was not unstudied in the great poem of his country, recollected that one of the ancestors of this family, and perhaps an occupant of this very mansion, had been pictured by Dante as a partaker of the immortal agonies of his Inferno. These reminiscences and associations, together with the tendency to heartbreak natural to a young man for the first time out of his native sphere, caused Giovanni to sigh heavily as he looked around the desolate and ill-furnished apartment.

"Holy Virgin, signor!" cried old Dame Lisabetta, who, won by the youth's remarkable beauty of person, was kindly endeavoring to give the chamber a habitable air, "what a sigh was that to come out of a young man's heart! Do you find this old mansion gloomy? For the love of Heaven, then, put your head out of the window, and you will see as bright sunshine as you have left in Naples."

Guasconti mechanically did as the old woman advised, but could not quite agree with her that the Paduan sunshine was as cheerful as that of southern Italy. Such as it was, however, it fell upon a garden beneath the window and expended its fostering influences on a variety of plants, which seemed to have been cultivated with exceeding care.

"Does this garden belong to the house?" asked Giovanni.

"Heaven forbid, signor, unless it were fruitful of better pot herbs than any that grow there now," answered old Lisabetta. "No; that garden is cultivated by the own hands of Signor Giacomo Rappaccini, the famous doctor, who, I warrant him, has been heard of as far as Naples. It is said that he distills these plants into medicines that are as potent as a charm. Oftentimes you may see the signor doctor at work, and perchance the signora, his daughter, too, gathering the strange flowers that grow in the garden."

The old woman had now done what she could for the aspect of the chamber; and, commending the young man to the protection of the saints, took her departure.

Giovanni still found no better occupation than to look down into the garden beneath his window. From its appearance, he judged it to be one of those botanic gardens which were of earlier date in Padua than elsewhere in Italy or in the world. Or, not improbably, it might once have been the pleasure-place of an opulent family; for there was the ruin of a marble fountain in the centre, sculptured with rare art, but so woefully shattered that it was impossible to trace the original design from the chaos of remaining fragments. The water, however, continued to gush and sparkle into the sunbeams as cheerfully as ever. A little gurgling sound ascended to the young man's window, and made him feel as if the fountain were an immortal spirit that sung its song unceasingly and without heeding the vicissitudes around it, while one century embodied it in marble and another scattered the perishable garniture on the soil. All about the pool into which the water subsided grew various plants, that seemed to require a plentiful supply of moisture for the nourishment of gigantic leaves, and in some instances, flowers gorgeously magnificent. There was one shrub in particular, set in a marble vase in the midst of the pool, that bore a profusion of purple blossoms, each of which had the lustre and richness of a gem; and the whole together made a show so resplendent that it seemed enough to illuminate the garden, even had there been no sunshine. Every portion of the soil was peopled with plants and herbs, which, if less beautiful, still bore tokens of assiduous care, as if all had their individual virtues, known to the scientific mind that fostered them. Some were placed in urns, rich with old carving, and others in common garden pots; some crept serpent-like along the ground or climbed on high, using whatever means of ascent was offered them. One plant had wreathed itself round a statue of Vertumnus, which was thus quite veiled and shrouded in a drapery of hanging foliage, so happily arranged that it might have served a sculptor for a study.

While Giovanni stood at the window he heard a rustling behind a screen of leaves, and became aware that a person was at work in the garden. His figure soon emerged into view, and showed itself to be that of no common laborer, but a tall, emaciated, sallow, and sickly-looking man, dressed in a scholar's garb of black. He was beyond the middle term of life, with gray hair, a thin, gray beard, and a face singularly marked with intellect and cultivation, but which could never, even in his more youthful days, have expressed much warmth of heart.

Nothing could exceed the intentness with which this scientific gardener examined every shrub which grew in his path: it seemed as if he was looking into their inmost nature, making observations in regard to their creative essence, and discovering why one leaf grew in this shape and another in that, and wherefore such and such flowers differed among themselves in hue and perfume. Nevertheless, in spite of this deep intelligence on his part, there was no approach to intimacy between himself and these vegetable existences. On the contrary, he avoided their actual touch or the direct inhaling of their odors with a caution that impressed Giovanni most disagreeably; for the man's demeanor was that of one walking among malignant influences, such as savage beasts, or deadly snakes, or evil spirits, which, should he allow them one moment of license, would wreak upon him some terrible fatality. It was strangely frightful to the young man's imagination to see this air of insecurity in a person cultivating a garden, that most simple and innocent of human toils, and which had been alike the joy and labor of the unfallen parents of the race. Was this garden, then, the Eden of the present world? And this man, with such a perception of harm in what his own hands caused to grow,—was he the Adam?

The distrustful gardener, while plucking away the dead leaves or pruning the too luxuriant growth of the shrubs, defended his hands with a pair of thick gloves. Nor were these his only armor. When, in his walk through the garden, he came to the magnificent plant that hung its purple gems beside the marble fountain, he placed a kind of mask over his mouth and nostrils, as if all this beauty did but conceal a deadlier malice;

but, finding his task still too dangerous, he drew back, removed the mask, and called loudly, but in the infirm voice of a person affected with inward disease,—

"Beatrice! Beatrice!"

"Here am I, my father. What would you?" cried a rich and youthful voice from the window of the opposite house—a voice as rich as a tropical sunset, and which made Giovanni, though he knew not why, think of deep hues of purple or crimson and of perfumes heavily delectable. "Are you in the garden?"

"Yes, Beatrice," answered the gardener, "and I need your help."

Soon there emerged from under a sculptured portal the figure of a young girl, arrayed with as much richness of taste as the most splendid of the flowers, beautiful as the day, and with a bloom so deep and vivid that one shade more would have been too much. She looked redundant with life, health, and energy; all of which attributes were bound down and compressed, as it were, and girdled tensely, in their luxuriance, by her virgin zone. Yet Giovanni's fancy must have grown morbid while he looked down into the garden; for the impression which the fair stranger made upon him was as if here were another flower, the human sister of those vegetable ones, as beautiful as they, more beautiful than the richest of them, but still to be touched only with a glove, nor to be approached without a mask. As Beatrice came down the garden path, it was observable that she handled and inhaled the odor of several of the plants which her father had most sedulously avoided.

"Here, Beatrice," said the latter, "see how many needful offices require to be done to our chief treasure. Yet, shattered as I am, my life might pay the penalty of approaching it so closely as circumstances demand. Henceforth, I fear, this plant must be consigned to your sole charge."

"And gladly will I undertake it," cried again the rich tones of the young lady, as she bent towards the magnificent plant and opened her arms as if to embrace it. "Yes, my sister, my splendor, it shall be Beatrice's task to nurse and serve thee; and thou shalt reward her with thy kisses and perfumed breath, which to her is as the breath of life."

Then, with all the tenderness in her manner that was so strikingly expressed in her words, she busied herself with such attentions as the plant seemed to require; and Giovanni, at his lofty window, rubbed his eyes and almost doubted whether it were a girl tending her favorite flower, or one sister performing the duties of affection to another. The scene soon terminated. Whether Dr. Rappaccini had finished his labors in the garden, or that his watchful eye had caught the stranger's face, he now took his daughter's arm and retired. Night was already closing in; oppressive exhalations seemed to proceed from the plants and steal upward past the open window; and Giovanni, closing the lattice, went to his couch and dreamed of a rich flower and beautiful girl. Flower and maiden were different, and yet the same, and fraught with some strange peril in either shape.

But there is an influence in the light of morning that tends to rectify whatever errors of fancy, or even of judgment, we may have incurred during the sun's decline, or among the shadows of the night, or in the less wholesome glow of moonshine. Giovanni's first movement, on starting from sleep, was to throw open the window and gaze down into the garden which his dreams had made so fertile of mysteries. He was surprised and a little ashamed to find how real and matter-of-fact an affair it proved to be, in the first rays of the sun which gilded the dew-drops that hung upon leaf and blossom, and, while giving a brighter beauty to each rare flower, brought everything within the limits of ordinary experience. The young man rejoiced that, in the heart of the barren city, he had the privilege of overlooking this spot of lovely and luxuriant vegetation. It would serve, he said to himself, as a symbolic language to keep him in communion with Nature. Neither the sickly and thoughtworn Dr. Giacomo Rappaccini, it is true, nor his brilliant daughter, were now visible; so that Giovanni could not determine how much of the singularity which he attributed to both was due to their own qualities and how much to his wonder-working fancy; but he was inclined to take a most rational view of the whole matter.

In the course of the day he paid his respects to Signor Pietro Baglioni, professor of medicine in the university, a physician of eminent repute to whom Giovanni had brought a letter of introduction. The professor was an elderly personage, apparently of genial nature, and habits that might almost be called jovial. He kept the young man to dinner, and made himself very agreeable by the freedom and liveliness of his conversation, especially when warmed by a flask or two of Tuscan wine. Giovanni, conceiving that men of science, inhabitants of the same city, must needs be on familiar terms with one another, took an opportunity to mention the name of Dr. Rappaccini. But the professor did not respond with so much cordiality as he had anticipated.

"Ill would it become a teacher of the divine art of medicine," said Professor Pietro Baglioni, in answer to a question of Giovanni, "to withhold due and well-considered praise of a physician so eminently skilled as Rappaccini; but, on the other hand, I should answer it but scantily to my conscience were I to permit a worthy youth like yourself, Signor Giovanni, the son of an ancient friend, to imbibe erroneous ideas respecting a man who might hereafter chance to hold your life and death in his hands. The truth is, our worshipful Dr. Rappaccini has as much science as any member of the faculty—with perhaps one single exception—in Padua, or all Italy; but there are certain grave objections to his professional character."

"And what are they?" asked the young man.

"Has my friend Giovanni any disease of body or heart, that he is so inquisitive about physicians?" said the professor, with a smile. "But as for Rappaccini, it is said of him—and I, who know the man well, can answer for its truth—that he cares infinitely more for science than for mankind. His patients are interesting to him only as subjects for some new experiment. He would sacrifice human life, his own among the rest, or whatever else was dearest to him, for the sake of adding so much as a grain of mustard seed to the great heap of his accumulated knowledge."

"Methinks he is an awful man indeed," remarked Guasconti, mentally recalling the cold and purely intellectual aspect of Rappaccini. "And yet, worshipful professor, is it not a noble spirit? Are there many men capable of so spiritual a love of science?"

"God forbid," answered the professor, somewhat testily; "at least, unless they take sounder views of the healing art than those adopted by Rappaccini. It is his theory that all medicinal virtues are comprised within those substances which we term vegetable poisons. These he cultivates with his own hands, and is said even to have produced new varieties of poison, more horribly deleterious than Nature, without the assistance of this learned person, would ever have plagued the world withal. That the signor doctor does less mischief than might be expected with such dangerous substances is undeniable. Now and then, it must be owned, he has effected, or seemed to effect, a marvellous cure; but, to tell you my private mind, Signor Giovanni, he should receive little credit for such instances of success,—they being probably the work of chance,—but should be held strictly accountable for his failures, which may justly be considered his own work."

The youth might have taken Baglioni's opinions with many grains of allowance had he known that there was a professional warfare of long continuance between him and Dr. Rappaccini, in which the latter was generally thought to have gained the advantage. If the reader be inclined to judge for himself, we refer him to certain black-letter tracts on both sides, preserved in the medical department of the University of Padua.

"I know not, most learned professor," returned Giovanni, after musing on what had been said of Rappaccini's exclusive zeal for science,—"I know not how dearly this physician may love his art; but surely there is one object more dear to him. He has a daughter."

"Aha!" cried the professor, with a laugh. "So now our friend Giovanni's secret is out. You have heard of this daughter, whom all the young men in Padua are wild about, though not half a dozen have ever had the good hap to see her face. I know little of the Signora Beatrice save that Rappaccini is said to have instructed her deeply in his science, and that, young and beautiful as fame reports her, she is already qualified to fill a professor's chair. Perchance her father destines her for mine! Other absurd rumors there be, not worth talking about or listening to. So now, Signor Giovanni, drink off your glass of lachryma."

Guasconti returned to his lodgings somewhat heated with the wine he had quaffed, and which caused his brain to swim with strange fantasies in reference to Dr. Rappaccini and the beautiful Beatrice. On his way, happening to pass by a florist's, he bought a fresh bouquet of flowers.

Ascending to his chamber, he seated himself near the window, but within the shadow thrown by the depth of the wall, so that he could look down into the garden with little risk of being discovered. All beneath his eye was a solitude. The strange plants were basking in the sunshine, and now and then nodding gently to one another, as if in acknowledgment of sympathy and kindred. In the midst, by the shattered fountain, grew the magnificent shrub, with its purple gems clustering all over it; they glowed in the air, and gleamed back again out of the depths of the pool, which thus seemed to overflow with colored radiance from the rich reflection that was steeped in it. At first, as we have said, the garden was a solitude. Soon, however,—as Giovanni had half hoped, half feared, would be the case,—a figure appeared beneath the antique sculptured portal, and came down between the rows of plants, inhaling their various perfumes as if she were one of those beings of old classic fable that lived upon sweet odors. On again beholding Beatrice, the young man was even startled to perceive how much her beauty exceeded his recollection of it; so brilliant, so vivid, was its character, that she glowed amid the sunlight, and, as Giovanni whispered to himself, positively illuminated the more shadowy intervals of the garden path. Her face being now more revealed than on the former occasion, he was struck by its expression of simplicity and sweetness,—qualities that had not entered into his idea of her character, and which made him ask anew what manner of mortal she might be. Nor did he fail again to observe, or imagine, an analogy between the beautiful girl and the gorgeous shrub that hung its gemlike flowers over the fountain,—a resemblance which Beatrice seemed to have indulged a fantastic humor in heightening, both by the arrangement of her dress and the selection of its hues.

Approaching the shrub, she threw open her arms, as with a passionate ardor, and drew its branches into an intimate embrace—so intimate that her features were hidden in its leafy bosom and her glistening ringlets all intermingled with the flowers.

"Give me thy breath, my sister," exclaimed Beatrice; "for I am faint with common air. And give me this flower of thine, which I separate with gentlest fingers from the stem and place it close beside my heart."

With these words the beautiful daughter of Rappaccini plucked one of the richest blossoms of the shrub, and was about to fasten it in her bosom. But now, unless Giovanni's draughts of wine had bewildered his senses, a singular accident occurred. A small orange-colored reptile, of the lizard or chameleon species, chanced to be creeping along the path, just at the feet of Beatrice. It appeared to Giovanni,—but, at the distance from which he gazed, he could scarcely have seen anything so minute,—it appeared to him, however, that a drop or two of moisture from the broken stem of the flower descended upon the lizard's head. For an instant the reptile contorted itself violently, and then lay motionless in the sunshine. Beatrice observed this remarkable phenomenon, and crossed herself, sadly, but without surprise; nor did she therefore hesitate to arrange the fatal flower in her bosom. There it blushed, and almost glimmered with the dazzling effect of a precious stone, adding to her dress and aspect the one appropriate charm which nothing else in the world could have supplied. But Giovanni, out of the shadow of his window, bent forward and shrank back, and murmured and trembled.

"Am I awake? Have I my senses" said he to himself. "What is this being? Beautiful shall I call her, or inexpressibly terrible?"

Beatrice now strayed carelessly through the garden, approaching closer beneath Giovanni's window, so that he was compelled to thrust his head quite out of its concealment in order to gratify the intense and painful curiosity which she excited. At this moment there came a beautiful insect over the garden wall; it had, perhaps, wandered through the city, and found no flowers or verdure among those antique haunts of men until the heavy perfumes of Dr. Rappaccini's shrubs had lured it from afar. Without alighting on the flowers, this winged brightness seemed to be attracted by Beatrice, and lingered in the air and fluttered about her head. Now, here it could not be but that Giovanni Guasconti's eyes deceived him. Be that as it might, he fancied that, while Beatrice was gazing at the insect with childish delight, it grew faint and fell at her feet; its bright wings shivered; it was dead—from no cause that he could discern, unless it were the atmosphere of her breath. Again Beatrice crossed herself and sighed heavily as she bent over the dead insect.

An impulsive movement of Giovanni drew her eyes to the window. There she beheld the beautiful head of the young man—rather a Grecian than an Italian head, with fair, regular features, and a glistening of gold among his ringlets—gazing down upon her like a being that hovered in mid-air. Scarcely knowing what he did, Giovanni threw down the bouquet which he had hitherto held in his hand.

"Signora," said he, "there are pure and healthful flowers. Wear them for the sake of Giovanni Guasconti."

"Thanks, signor," replied Beatrice, with her rich voice, that came forth as it were like a gush of music, and with a mirthful expression half childish and half woman-like. "I accept your gift, and would fain recompense it with this precious purple flower; but if I toss it into the air it will not reach you. So Signor Guasconti must even content himself with my thanks."

She lifted the bouquet from the ground, and then, as if inwardly ashamed at having stepped aside from her maidenly reserve to respond to a stranger's greeting, passed swiftly homeward through the garden. But few as the moments were, it seemed to Giovanni, when she was on the point of vanishing beneath the sculptured portal, that his beautiful bouquet was already beginning to wither in her grasp. It was an idle thought; there could be no possibility of distinguishing a faded flower from a fresh one at so great a distance.

For many days after this incident the young man avoided the window that looked into Dr. Rappaccini's garden, as if something ugly and monstrous would have blasted his eyesight had he been betrayed into a glance. He felt conscious of having put himself, to a certain extent, within the influence of an unintelligible power by the communication which he had opened with Beatrice. The wisest course would have been, if his heart were in any real danger, to quit his lodgings and Padua itself at once; the next wiser, to have accustomed himself, as far as possible, to the familiar and daylight view of Beatrice—thus bringing her rigidly and systematically within the limits of ordinary experience. Least of all, while avoiding her sight, ought Giovanni to have remained so near this extraordinary being that the proximity and possibility even of intercourse should give a kind of substance and reality to the wild vagaries which his imagination ran riot continually in producing. Guasconti had not a deep heart—or, at all events, its depths were not sounded now; but he had a quick fancy, and an ardent southern temperament, which rose every instant to a higher fever pitch. Whether or no Beatrice possessed those terrible attributes, that fatal breath, the affinity with those so beautiful and deadly flowers which were indicated by what Giovanni had witnessed, she had at least instilled a fierce and subtle poison into his system. It was not love, although her rich beauty was a madness to him; nor horror, even while he fancied her spirit to be imbued with the same baneful essence that seemed to pervade her physical frame; but a wild offspring of both love and horror that had each parent in it, and burned like one and shivered like the other. Giovanni knew not what to dread; still less did he know what to hope; yet hope and dread kept a continual warfare in his breast, alternately vanquishing one another and starting up afresh to renew the contest. Blessed are all simple emotions, be they dark or bright! It is the lurid intermixture of the two that produces the illuminating blaze of the infernal regions.

Sometimes he endeavored to assuage the fever of his spirit by a rapid walk through the streets of Padua or beyond its gates: his footsteps kept time with the throbbings of his brain, so that the walk was apt to accelerate itself to a race. One day he found himself arrested; his arm was seized by a portly personage, who had turned back on recognizing the young man and expended much breath in overtaking him.

"Signor Giovanni! Stay, my young friend!" cried he. "Have you forgotten me? That might well be the case if I were as much altered as yourself."

It was Baglioni, whom Giovanni had avoided ever since their first meeting, from a doubt that the professor's sagacity would look too deeply into his secrets. Endeavoring to recover himself, he stared forth wildly from his inner world into the outer one and spoke like a man in a dream.

"Yes; I am Giovanni Guasconti. You are Professor Pietro Baglioni. Now let me pass!"

"Not yet, not yet, Signor Giovanni Guasconti," said the professor, smiling, but at the same time scrutinizing the youth with an earnest glance. "What! did I grow up side by side with your father? and shall his son pass me like a stranger in these old streets of

Padua? Stand still, Signor Giovanni; for we must have a word or two before we part."

"Speedily, then, most worshipful professor, speedily," said Giovanni with feverish impatience. "Does not your worship see that I am in haste?"

Now, while he was speaking there came a man in black along the street, stooping and moving feebly like a person in inferior health. His face was all overspread with a most sickly and sallow hue, but yet so pervaded with an expression of piercing and active intellect that an observer might easily have overlooked the merely physical attributes and have seen only this wonderful energy. As he passed, this person exchanged a cold and distant salutation with Baglioni, but fixed his eyes upon Giovanni with an intentness that seemed to bring out whatever was within him worthy of notice. Nevertheless, there was a peculiar quietness in the look, as if taking merely a speculative, not a human interest, in the young man.

"It is Dr. Rappaccini!" whispered the professor when the stranger had passed. "Has he ever seen your face before?"

"Not that I know," answered Giovanni, starting at the name.

"He *has* seen you! he must have seen you!" said Baglioni, hastily. "For some purpose or other, this man of science is making a study of you. I know that look of his! It is the same that coldly illuminates his face as he bends over a bird, a mouse, or a butterfly, which, in pursuance of some experiment, he has killed by the perfume of a flower; a look as deep as Nature itself, but without Nature's warmth of love. Signor Giovanni, I will stake my life upon it, you are the subject of one of Rappaccini's experiments!"

"Will you make a fool of me?" cried Giovanni passionately. "*That*, signor professor, were an untoward experiment."

"Patience! patience!" replied the imperturbable professor. "I tell thee, my poor Giovanni, that Rappaccini has a scientific interest in thee. Thou hast fallen into fearful hands! And the Signora Beatrice,—what part does she act in this mystery?"

But Guasconti, finding Baglioni's pertinacity intolerable, here broke away, and was gone before the professor could again seize his arm. He looked after the young man intently and shook his head.

"This must not be," said Baglioni to himself. "The youth is the son of my old friend, and shall not come to any harm from which the arcana of medical science can preserve him. Besides, it is too insufferable an impertinence in Rappaccini, thus to snatch the lad out of my own hands, as I may say, and make use of him for his infernal experiments. This daughter of his! It shall be looked to. Perchance, most learned Rappaccini, I may foil you where you little dream of it!"

Meanwhile Giovanni had pursued a circuitous route, and at length found himself at the door of his lodgings. As he crossed the threshold he was met by old Lisabetta, who smirked and smiled, and was evidently desirous to attract his attention; vainly, however, as the ebullition of his feelings had momentarily subsided into a cold and dull vacuity. He turned his eyes full upon the withered face that was puckering itself into a smile, but seemed to behold it not. The old dame, therefore, laid her grasp upon his cloak.

"Signor! signor!" whispered she, still with a smile over the whole breadth of her visage, so that it looked not unlike a grotesque carving in wood, darkened by centuries. "Listen, signor! There is a private entrance into the garden!"

"What do you say?" exclaimed Giovanni, turning quickly about, as if an inanimate thing should start into feverish life. "A private entrance into Dr. Rappaccini's garden?"

"Hush! hush! not so loud!" whispered Lisabetta, putting her hand over his mouth. "Yes; into the worshipful doctor's garden, where you may see all his fine shrubbery. Many a young man in Padua would give gold to be admitted among those flowers."

Giovanni put a piece of gold into her hand.

"Show me the way," said he.

A surmise, probably excited by his conversation with Baglioni, crossed his mind, that this interposition of old Lisabetta might perchance be connected with the intrigue, whatever were its nature, in which the professor seemed to suppose that Dr. Rappaccini was involving him. But such a suspicion, though it disturbed Giovanni, was inadequate to restrain him. The instant that he was aware of the possibility of approaching Beatrice, it seemed an absolute necessity of his existence to do so. It mattered not whether she were angel or demon; he was irrevocably within her sphere, and must obey the law that whirled him onward, in ever-lessening circles, towards a result which he did not attempt to foreshadow; and yet, strange to say, there came across him a sudden doubt whether this intense interest on his part were not delusory; whether it were really of so deep and positive a nature as to justify him in now thrusting himself into an incalculable position; whether it were not merely the fantasy of a young man's brain, only slightly or not at all connected with his heart.

He paused, hesitated, turned half about, but again went on. His withered guide led him along several obscure passages, and finally undid a door, through which, as it was opened, there came the sight and sound of rustling leaves, with the broken sunshine glimmering among them. Giovanni stepped forth, and, forcing himself through the entanglement of a shrub that wreathed its tendrils over the hidden entrance, stood beneath his own window in the open area of Dr. Rappaccini's garden.

How often is it the case that, when impossibilities have come to pass and dreams have condensed their misty substance into tangible realities, we find ourselves calm, and even coldly self-possessed, amid circumstances which it would have been a delirium of joy or agony to anticipate! Fate delights to thwart us thus. Passion will choose his own time to rush upon the scene, and lingers sluggishly behind when an appropriate adjustment of events would seem to summon his appearance. So was it now with Giovanni. Day after day his pulses had throbbed with feverish blood at the improbable idea of an interview with Beatrice, and of standing with her, face to face, in this very garden, basking in the Oriental sunshine of her beauty, and snatching from her full gaze the mystery which he deemed the riddle of his own existence. But now there was a singular and untimely equanimity within his breast. He threw a glance around the garden to discover if Beatrice or her father were present, and, perceiving that he was alone, began a critical observation of the plants.

The aspect of one and all of them dissatisfied him; their gorgeousness seemed fierce, passionate, and even unnatural. There was hardly an individual shrub which a wanderer, straying by himself through a forest, would not have been startled to find growing wild, as if an unearthly face had glared at him out of the thicket. Several also would have shocked a delicate instinct by an appearance of artificialness indicating that there had been such commixture, and, as it were, adultery, of various vegetable species, that the production was no longer of God's making, but the monstrous offspring of man's depraved fancy, glowing with only an evil mockery of beauty. They were probably the result of experiment, which in one or two cases had succeeded in mingling plants individually lovely into a compound possessing the questionable and ominous character that distinguished the whole growth of the garden. In fine, Giovanni recognized but two or three plants in the collection, and those of a kind that he well knew to be poisonous. While busy with these contemplations he heard the rustling of a silken garment, and, turning, beheld Beatrice emerging from beneath the sculptured portal.

Giovanni had not considered with himself what should be his deportment; whether he should apologize for his intrusion into the garden, or assume that he was there with the privity at least, if not by the desire, of Dr. Rappaccini or his daughter; but Beatrice's manner placed him at his ease, though leaving him still in doubt by what agency he had gained admittance. She came lightly along the path and met him near the broken fountain. There was surprise in her face, but brightened by a simple and kind expression of pleasure.

"You are a connoisseur in flowers, signor," said Beatrice, with a smile, alluding to the bouquet which he had flung her from the window. "It is no marvel, therefore, if the sight of my father's rare collection has tempted you to take a nearer view. If he were here, he could tell you many strange and interesting facts as to the nature and habits of these shrubs; for he has spent a lifetime in such studies, and this garden is his world."

"And yourself, lady," observed Giovanni, "if fame says true,—you likewise are deeply skilled in the virtues indicated by these rich blossoms and these spicy perfumes. Would you deign to be my instructress, I should prove an apter scholar than if taught by Signor Rappaccini himself."

"Are there such idle rumors?" asked Beatrice, with the music of a pleasant laugh. "Do people say that I am skilled in my father's science of plants? What a jest is there! No; though I have grown up among these flowers, I know no more of them than their hues and perfume;

and sometimes methinks I would fain rid myself of even that small knowledge. There are many flowers here, and those not the least brilliant, that shock and offend me when they meet my eye. But pray, signor, do not believe these stories about my science. Believe nothing of me save what you see with your own eyes."

"And must I believe all that I have seen with my own eyes?" asked Giovanni, pointedly, while the recollection of former scenes make him shrink. "No, signora; you demand too little of me. Bid me believe nothing save what comes from your own lips."

It would appear that Beatrice understood him. There came a deep flush to her cheek; but she looked full into Giovanni's eyes, and responded to his gaze of uneasy suspicion with a queenlike haughtiness.

"I do so bid you, signor," she replied. "Forget whatever you may have fancied in regard to me. If true to the outward senses, still it may be false in its essence; but the words of Beatrice Rappaccini's lips are true from the depths of the heart outward. Those you may believe."

A fervor glowed in her whole aspect and beamed upon Giovanni's consciousness like the light of truth itself; but while she spoke there was a fragrance in the atmosphere around her, rich and delightful, though evanescent, yet which the young man, from an indefinable reluctance, scarcely dared to draw into his lungs. It might be the odor of the flowers. Could it be Beatrice's breath which thus embalmed her words with a strange richness, as if by steeping them in her heart? A faintness passed like a shadow over Giovanni and flitted away; he seemed to gaze through the beautiful girl's eyes into her transparent soul, and felt no more doubt or fear.

The tinge of passion that had colored Beatrice's manner vanished; she became gay, and appeared to derive a pure delight from her communion with the youth not unlike what the maiden of a lonely island might have felt conversing with a voyager from the civilized world. Evidently her experience of life had been confined within the limits of that garden. She talked now about matters as simple as the daylight or summer clouds, and now asked questions in reference to the city, or Giovanni's distant home, his friends, his mother, and his sisters—questions indicating such seclusion, and such lack of familiarity with modes and forms, that Giovanni responded as if to an infant. Her spirit gushed out before him like a fresh rill that was just catching its first glimpse of the sunlight and wondering at the reflections of earth and sky which were flung into its bosom. There came thoughts, too, from a deep source, and fantasies of a gemlike brilliancy, as if diamonds and rubies sparkled upward among the bubbles of the fountain. Ever and anon there gleamed across the young man's mind a sense of wonder that he should be walking side by side with the being who had so wrought upon his imagination, whom he had idealized in such hues of terror, in whom he had positively witnessed such manifestations of dreadful attributes,—that he should be conversing with Beatrice like a brother, and should find her so human and so maidenlike. But such reflections were only momentary; the effect of her character was too real not to make itself familiar at once.

In this free intercourse they had strayed through the garden, and now, after many turns among its avenues, were come to the shattered fountain, beside which grew the magnificent shrub, with its treasury of glowing blossoms. A fragrance was diffused from it which Giovanni recognized as identical with that which he had attributed to Beatrice's breath, but incomparably more powerful. As her eyes fell upon it, Giovanni beheld her press her hand to her bosom as if her heart were throbbing suddenly and painfully.

"For the first time in my life," murmured she, addressing the shrub, "I had forgotten thee."

"I remember, signora" said Giovanni "that you once promised to reward me with one of these living gems for the bouquet which I had the happy boldness to fling to your feet. Permit me now to pluck it as a memorial of this interview."

He made a step towards the shrub with extended hand; but Beatrice darted forward uttering a shriek that went through his heart like a dagger. She caught his hand and drew it back with the whole force of her slender figure. Giovanni felt her touch thrilling through his fibres.

"Touch it not!" exclaimed she in a voice of agony. "Not for thy life! It is fatal!"

Then hiding her face she fled from him and vanished beneath the sculptured portal. As Giovanni followed her with his eyes he beheld the emaciated figure and pale intelligence of Dr. Rappaccini, who had been watching the scene he knew not how long, within the shadow of the entrance.

No sooner was Guasconti alone in his chamber than the image of Beatrice came back to his passionate musings, invested with all the witchery that had been gathering around it ever since his first glimpse of her, and now likewise imbued with a tender warmth of girlish womanhood. She was human; her nature was endowed with all gentle and feminine qualities; she was worthiest to be worshipped; she was capable, surely, on her part, of the height and heroism of love. Those tokens which he had hitherto considered as proofs of a frightful peculiarity in her physical and moral system were now either forgotten, or, by the subtle sophistry of passion transmitted into a golden crown of enchantment, rendering Beatrice the more admirable by so much as she was the more unique. Whatever had looked ugly was now beautiful; or, if incapable of such a change, it stole away and hid itself among those shapeless half ideas which throng the dim region beyond the daylight of our perfect consciousness. Thus did he spend the night, nor fell asleep until the dawn had begun to awaken the slumbering flowers in Dr. Rappaccini's garden, whither Giovanni's dreams doubtless led him. Up rose the sun in his due season, and, flinging his beams upon the young man's eyelids, awoke him to a sense of pain. When thoroughly aroused, he became sensible of a burning and tingling agony in his hand—in his right hand—the very hand which Beatrice had grasped in her own when he was on the point of plucking one of the gemlike flowers. On the back of that hand there was now a purple print like that of four small fingers, and the likeness of a slender thumb upon his wrist.

Oh, how stubbornly does love,—or even that cunning semblance of love which flourishes in the imagination, but strikes no depth of root into the heart,—how stubbornly does it hold its faith until the moment comes when it is doomed to vanish into thin mist! Giovanni wrapped a handkerchief about his hand and wondered what evil thing had stung him, and soon forgot his pain in a reverie of Beatrice.

After the first interview, a second was in the inevitable course of what we call fate. A third; a fourth; and a meeting with Beatrice in the garden was no longer an incident in Giovanni's daily life, but the whole space in which he might be said to live; for the anticipation and memory of that ecstatic hour made up the remainder. Nor was it otherwise with the daughter of Rappaccini. She watched for the youth's appearance, and flew to his side with confidence as unreserved as if they had been playmates from early infancy—as if they were such playmates still. If, by any unwonted chance, he failed to come at the appointed moment, she stood beneath the window and sent up the rich sweetness of her tones to float around him in his chamber and echo and reverberate throughout his heart: "Giovanni! Giovanni! Why tarriest thou? Come down!" And down he hastened into that Eden of poisonous flowers.

But, with all this intimate familiarity, there was still a reserve in Beatrice's demeanor, so rigidly and invariably sustained that the idea of infringing it scarcely occurred to his imagination. By all appreciable signs, they loved; they had looked love with eyes that conveyed the holy secret from the depths of one soul into the depths of the other, as if it were too sacred to be whispered by the way; they had even spoken love in those gushes of passion when their spirits darted forth in articulated breath like tongues of long-hidden flame; and yet there had been no seal of lips, no clasp of hands, nor any slightest caress such as love claims and hallows. He had never touched one of the gleaming ringlets of her hair; her garment—so marked was the physical barrier between them—had never been waved against him by a breeze. On the few occasions when Giovanni had seemed tempted to overstep the limit, Beatrice grew so sad, so stern, and withal wore such a look of desolate separation, shuddering at itself, that not a spoken word was requisite to repel him. At such times he was startled at the horrible suspicions that rose, monster-like, out of the caverns of his heart and stared him in the face; his love grew thin and faint as the morning mist, his doubts alone had substance. But, when Beatrice's face brightened again after the momentary shadow, she was transformed at once from the mysterious, questionable being whom he had watched with so much awe and horror; she was now the beautiful and unsophisticated girl whom he felt that his spirit knew with a certainty beyond all other knowledge.

A considerable time had now passed since Giovanni's last meeting with Baglioni. One morning, however, he was disagreeably surprised by a visit from the professor, whom he had scarcely thought of for whole weeks, and would willingly have forgotten still longer. Given up as he had long been to a pervading excitement, he could tolerate no companions except upon condition of their perfect sympathy with his present state of feeling. Such sympathy was not to be expected from Professor Baglioni.

The visitor chatted carelessly for a few moments about the gossip of the city and the university, and then took up another topic.

"I have been reading an old classic author lately," said he, "and met with a story that strangely interested me. Possibly you may remember it. It is of an Indian prince, who sent a beautiful woman as a present to Alexander the Great. She was as lovely as the dawn and gorgeous as the sunset; but what especially distinguished her was a certain rich perfume in her breath—richer than a garden of Persian roses. Alexander, as was natural to a youthful conqueror, fell in love at first sight with this magnificent stranger; but a certain sage physician, happening to be present, discovered a terrible secret in regard to her."

"And what was that?" asked Giovanni, turning his eyes downward to avoid those of the professor.

"That this lovely woman," continued Baglioni, with emphasis, "had been nourished with poisons from her birth upward, until her whole nature was so imbued with them that she herself had become the deadliest poison in existence. Poison was her element of life. With that rich perfume of her breath she blasted the very air. Her love would have been poison—her embrace death. Is not this a marvellous tale?"

"A childish fable," answered Giovanni, nervously starting from his chair. "I marvel how your worship finds time to read such nonsense among your graver studies."

"By the by," said the professor, looking uneasily about him, "what singular fragrance is this in your apartment? Is it the perfume of your gloves? It is faint, but delicious; and yet, after all, by no means agreeable. Were I to breathe it long, methinks it would make me ill. It is like the breath of a flower; but I see no flowers in the chamber."

"Nor are there any," replied Giovanni, who had turned pale as the professor spoke; "nor, I think, is there any fragrance except in your worship's imagination. Odors, being a sort of element combined of the sensual and the spiritual, are apt to deceive us in this manner. The recollection of a perfume, the bare idea of it, may easily be mistaken for a present reality."

"Ay; but my sober imagination does not often play such tricks," said Baglioni; "and, were I to fancy any kind of odor, it would be that of some vile apothecary drug, wherewith my fingers are likely enough to be imbued. Our worshipful friend Rappaccini, as I have heard, tinctures his medicaments with odors richer than those of Araby. Doubtless, likewise, the fair and learned Signora Beatrice would minister to her patients with draughts as sweet as a maiden's breath; but woe to him that sips them!"

Giovanni's face evinced many contending emotions. The tone in which the professor alluded to the pure and lovely daughter of Rappaccini was a torture to his soul; and yet the intimation of a view of her character, opposite to his own, gave instantaneous distinctness to a thousand dim suspicions, which now grinned at him like so many demons. But he strove hard to quell them and to respond to Baglioni with a true lover's perfect faith.

"Signor professor," said he, "you were my father's friend; perchance, too, it is your purpose to act a friendly part towards his son. I would fain feel nothing towards you save respect and deference; but I pray you to observe, signor, that there is one subject on which we must not speak. You know not the Signora Beatrice. You cannot, therefore, estimate the wrong—the blasphemy, I may even say—that is offered to her character by a light or injurious word."

"Giovanni! my poor Giovanni!" answered the professor, with calm expression of pity, "I know this wretched girl far better than yourself. You shall hear the truth in respect to the poisoner Rappaccini and his poisonous daughter; yes, poisonous as she is beautiful. Listen; for, even should you do violence to my gray hairs, it shall not silence me. That old fable of the Indian woman has become a truth by the deep and deadly science of Rappaccini and in the person of the lovely Beatrice."

Giovanni groaned and hid his face.

"Her father," continued Baglioni, "was not restrained by natural affection from offering up his child in this horrible manner as the victim of his insane zeal for science; for, let us do him justice, he is as true a man of science as ever distilled his own heart in an alembic. What, then, will be your fate? Beyond a doubt you are selected as the material of some new experiment. Perhaps the result is to be death; perhaps a fate more awful still. Rappaccini, with what he calls the interest of science before his eyes, will hesitate at nothing."

"It is a dream," muttered Giovanni to himself; "surely it is a dream."

"But," resumed the professor, "be of good cheer, son of my friend. It is not yet too late for the rescue. Possibly we may even succeed in bringing back this miserable child within the limits of ordinary nature, from which her father's madness has estranged her. Behold this little silver vase! It was wrought by the hands of the renowned Benvenuto Cellini, and is well worthy to be a love gift to the fairest dame in Italy. But its contents are invaluable. One little sip of this antidote would have rendered the most virulent poisons of the Borgias innocuous. Doubt not that it will be as efficacious against those of Rappaccini. Bestow the vase, and the precious liquid within it, on your Beatrice, and hopefully await the result."

Baglioni laid a small, exquisitely wrought silver vial on the table and withdrew, leaving what he had said to produce its effect upon the young man's mind.

"We will thwart Rappaccini yet," thought he, chuckling to himself, as he descended the stairs; "but, let us confess the truth of him, he is a wonderful man—a wonderful man indeed; a vile empiric, however, in his practice, and therefore not to be tolerated by those who respect the good old rules of the medical profession."

Throughout Giovanni's whole acquaintance with Beatrice, he had occasionally, as we have said, been haunted by dark surmises as to her character; yet so thoroughly had she made herself felt by him as a simple, natural, most affectionate, and guileless creature, that the image now held up by Professor Baglioni looked as strange and incredible as if it were not in accordance with his own original conception. True, there were ugly recollections connected with his first glimpses of the beautiful girl; he could not quite forget the bouquet that withered in her grasp, and the insect that perished amid the sunny air, by no ostensible agency save the fragrance of her breath. These incidents, however, dissolving in the pure light of her character, had no longer the efficacy of facts, but were acknowledged as mistaken fantasies, by whatever testimony of the senses they might appear to be substantiated. There is something truer and more real than what we can see with the eyes and touch with the finger. On such better evidence had Giovanni founded his confidence in Beatrice, though rather by the necessary force of her high attributes than by any deep and generous faith on his part. But now his spirit was incapable of sustaining itself at the height to which the early enthusiasm of passion had exalted it; he fell down, grovelling among earthly doubts, and defiled therewith the pure whiteness of Beatrice's image. Not that he gave her up; he did but distrust. He resolved to institute some decisive test that should satisfy him, once for all, whether there were those dreadful peculiarities in her physical nature which could not be supposed to exist without some corresponding monstrosity of soul. His eyes, gazing down afar, might have deceived him as to the lizard, the insect, and the flowers; but if he could witness, at the distance of a few paces, the sudden blight of one fresh and healthful flower in Beatrice's hand, there would be room for no further question. With this idea he hastened to the florist's and purchased a bouquet that was still gemmed with the morning dew-drops.

It was now the customary hour of his daily interview with Beatrice. Before descending into the garden, Giovanni failed not to look at his figure in the mirror,—a vanity to be expected in a beautiful young man, yet, as displaying itself at that troubled and feverish moment, the token of a certain shallowness of feeling and insincerity of character. He did gaze, however, and said to himself that his features had never before possessed so rich a grace, nor his eyes such vivacity, nor his cheeks so warm a hue of superabundant life.

"At least," thought he, "her poison has not yet insinuated itself into my system. I am no flower to perish in her grasp."

With that thought he turned his eyes on the bouquet, which he had never once laid aside from his hand. A thrill of indefinable horror shot through his frame on perceiving that those dewy flowers were already beginning to droop; they wore the aspect of things that had been fresh and lovely yesterday. Giovanni grew white as marble, and stood motionless before the mirror, staring at his own reflection there as at the likeness of something frightful. He remembered Baglioni's remark about the fragrance that seemed to pervade the chamber. It must have been the poison in his breath! Then he shuddered—shuddered at himself. Recovering from his stupor, he began to watch with curious eye a spider that was busily at work hanging its web from the antique cornice of the apartment, crossing and recrossing the artful system of interwoven lines—as vigorous and active a spider as ever dangled from an old ceiling. Giovanni bent towards the insect, and emitted a deep, long breath. The spider suddenly ceased its toil; the web vibrated with a tremor originating in the body of the small artisan. Again Giovanni sent forth a breath, deeper, longer, and imbued with a venomous feeling out of his heart: he knew not whether he were wicked, or only desperate. The spider made a convulsive gripe with his limbs and hung dead across the window.

"Accursed! accursed!" muttered Giovanni, addressing himself. "Hast thou grown so poisonous that this deadly insect perishes by thy breath?"

At that moment a rich, sweet voice came floating up from the garden.

"Giovanni! Giovanni! It is past the hour! Why tarriest thou? Come down!"

"Yes," muttered Giovanni again. "She is the only being whom my breath may not slay! Would that it might!"

He rushed down, and in an instant was standing before the bright and loving eyes of Beatrice. A moment ago his wrath and despair had been so fierce that he could have desired nothing so much as to wither her by a glance; but with her actual presence there came influences which had too real an existence to be at once shaken off: recollections of the delicate and benign power of her feminine nature, which had so often enveloped him in a religious calm; recollections of many a holy and passionate outgush of her heart, when the pure fountain had been unsealed from its depths and made visible in its transparency to his mental eye; recollections which, had Giovanni known how to estimate them, would have assured him that all this ugly mystery was but an earthly illusion, and that, whatever mist of evil might seem to have gathered over her, the real Beatrice was a heavenly angel. Incapable as he was of such high faith, still her presence had not utterly lost its magic. Giovanni's rage was quelled into an aspect of sullen insensibility. Beatrice, with a quick spiritual sense, immediately felt that there was a gulf of blackness between them which neither he nor she could pass. They walked on together, sad and silent, and came thus to the marble fountain and to its pool of water on the ground, in the midst of which grew the shrub that bore gem-like blossoms. Giovanni was affrighted at the eager enjoyment—the appetite, as it were—with which he found himself inhaling the fragrance of the flowers.

"Beatrice," asked he, abruptly, "whence came this shrub?"

"My father created it," answered she, with simplicity.

"Created it! created it!" repeated Giovanni. "What mean you, Beatrice?"

"He is a man fearfully acquainted with the secrets of Nature," replied Beatrice; "and, at the hour when I first drew breath, this plant sprang from the soil, the offspring of his science, of his intellect, while I was but his earthly child. Approach it not!" continued she, observing with terror that Giovanni was drawing nearer to the shrub. "It has qualities that you little dream of. But I, dearest Giovanni,—I grew up and blossomed with the plant and was nourished with its breath. It was my sister, and I loved it with a human affection; for, alas!—hast thou not suspected it?—there was an awful doom."

Here Giovanni frowned so darkly upon her that Beatrice paused and trembled. But her faith in his tenderness reassured her, and made her blush that she had doubted for an instant.

"There was an awful doom," she continued, "the effect of my father's fatal love of science, which estranged me from all society of my kind. Until Heaven sent thee, dearest Giovanni, oh, how lonely was thy poor Beatrice!"

"Was it a hard doom?" asked Giovanni, fixing his eyes upon her.

"Only of late have I known how hard it was," answered she, tenderly. "Oh, yes; but my heart was torpid, and therefore quiet."

Giovanni's rage broke forth from his sullen gloom like a lightning flash out of a dark cloud.

"Accursed one!" cried he, with venomous scorn and anger. "And, finding thy solitude wearisome, thou hast severed me likewise from all the warmth of life and enticed me into the region of unspeakable horror!"

"Giovanni!" exclaimed Beatrice, turning her large bright eyes upon his face. The force of his words had not found its way into her mind; she was merely thunderstruck.

"Yes, poisonous thing!" repeated Giovanni, beside himself with passion. "Thou hast done it! Thou has blasted me! Thou hast filled my veins with poison! Thou hast made me as hateful, as ugly, as loathsome and deadly a creature as thyself—a world's wonder of hideous monstrosity! Now, if our breath be happily as fatal to ourselves as to all others, let us join our lips in one kiss of unutterable hatred, and so die!"

"What has befallen me?" murmured Beatrice, with a low moan out of her heart. "Holy Virgin, pity me, a poor heartbroken child!"

"Thou,—dost thou pray?" cried Giovanni, still with the same fiendish scorn. "Thy very prayers as they come from thy lips, taint the atmosphere with death. Yes, yes; let us pray! Let us to church and dip our fingers in the holy water at the portal! They that come after us will perish as by a pestilence! Let us sign crosses in the air! It will be scattering curses abroad in the likeness of holy symbols!"

"Giovanni," said Beatrice, calmly, for her grief was beyond passion, "why dost thou join thyself with me thus in those terrible words? I, it is true, am the horrible thing thou namest me. But thou,—what hast thou to do, save with one other shudder at my hideous misery to go forth out of the garden and mingle with thy race, and forget there ever crawled on earth such a monster as poor Beatrice?"

"Dost thou pretend ignorance?" asked Giovanni, scowling upon her. "Behold this power have I gained from the pure daughter of Rappaccini."

There was a swarm of summer insects flitting through the air in search of the food promised by the flower odors of the fatal garden. They circled round Giovanni's head, and were evidently attracted towards him by the same influence which had drawn them for an instant within the sphere of several of the shrubs. He sent forth a breath among them, and smiled bitterly at Beatrice as at least a score of the insects fell dead upon the ground.

"I see it! I see it!" shrieked Beatrice. "It is my father's fatal science! No, no, Giovanni; it was not I!

Never! never! I dreamed only to love thee and be with thee a little time, and so to let thee pass away, leaving but thine image in mine heart; for, Giovanni, believe it, though my body be nourished with poison, my spirit is God's creature, and craves love as its daily food. But my father,—he has united us in this fearful sympathy. Yes; spurn me, tread upon me, kill me! Oh, what is death after such words as thine? But it was not I. Not for a world of bliss would I have done it."

Giovanni's passion had exhausted itself in its outburst from his lips. There now came across him a sense, mournful, and not without tenderness, of the intimate and peculiar relationship between Beatrice and himself. They stood, as it were, in an utter solitude, which would be made none the less solitary by the densest throng of human life. Ought not, then, the desert of humanity around them to press this insulated pair closer together? If they should be cruel to one another, who was there to be kind to them? Besides, thought Giovanni, might there not still be a hope of his returning within the limits of ordinary nature, and leading Beatrice, the redeemed Beatrice, by the hand? O, weak, and selfish, and unworthy spirit, that could dream of an earthly union and earthly happiness as possible, after such deep love had been so bitterly wronged as was Beatrice's love by Giovanni's blighting words! No, no; there could be no such hope. She must pass heavily, with that broken heart, across the borders of Time—she must bathe her hurts in some fount of paradise, and forget her grief in the light of immortality, and *there* be well.

But Giovanni did not know it.

"Dear Beatrice," said he, approaching her, while she shrank away as always at his approach, but now with a different impulse, "dearest Beatrice our fate is not yet so desperate. Behold! there is a medicine, potent, as a wise physician has assured me, and almost divine in its efficacy. It is composed of ingredients the most opposite to those by which thy awful father has brought this calamity upon thee and me. It is distilled of blessed herbs. Shall we not quaff it together, and thus be purified from evil?"

"Give it me!" said Beatrice, extending her hand to receive the little silver vial which Giovanni took from his bosom. She added, with a peculiar emphasis, "I will drink; but do thou await the result."

She put Baglioni's antidote to her lips; and, at the same moment, the figure of Rappaccini emerged from the portal and came slowly towards the marble fountain. As he drew near, the pale man of science seemed to gaze with a triumphant expression at the beautiful youth and maiden, as might an artist who should spend his life in achieving a picture or a group of statuary and finally be satisfied with his success. He paused; his bent form grew erect with conscious power; he spread out his hands over them in the attitude of a father imploring a blessing upon his children; but those were the same hands that had thrown poison into the stream of their lives. Giovanni trembled. Beatrice shuddered nervously, and pressed her hand upon her heart.

"My daughter," said Rappaccini, "thou art no longer lonely in the world. Pluck one of those precious gems from thy sister shrub and bid thy bridegroom wear it in his bosom. It will not harm him now. My science and the sympathy between thee and him have so wrought within his system that he now stands apart from common men, as thou dost, daughter of my pride and triumph, from ordinary women. Pass on, then, through the world, most dear to one another and dreadful to all besides!"

"My father," said Beatrice, feebly,—and still as she spoke she kept her hand upon her heart,—"wherefore didst thou inflict this miserable doom upon thy child?"

"Miserable!" exclaimed Rappaccini. "What mean you, foolish girl? Dost thou deem it misery to be endowed with marvellous gifts against which no power nor strength could avail an enemy—misery, to be able to quell the mightiest with a breath—misery, to be as terrible as thou art beautiful? Wouldst thou, then, have preferred the condition of a weak woman, exposed to all evil and capable of none?"

"I would fain have been loved, not feared," murmured Beatrice, sinking down upon the ground. "But now it matters not. I am going, father, where the evil which thou hast striven to mingle with my being will pass away like a dream—like the fragrance of these poisonous flowers, which will no longer taint my breath among the flowers of Eden. Farewell, Giovanni! Thy words of hatred are like lead within my heart; but they, too, will fall away as I ascend. Oh, was there not, from the first, more poison in thy nature than in mine?"

To Beatrice,—so radically had her earthly part been wrought upon by Rappaccini's skill,—as poison had been life, so the powerful antidote was death; and thus the poor victim of man's ingenuity and of thwarted nature, and of the fatality that attends all such efforts of perverted wisdom, perished there, at the feet of her father and Giovanni. Just at that moment Professor Pietro Baglioni looked forth from the window, and called loudly, in a tone of triumph mixed with horror, to the thunderstricken man of science,—

"Rappaccini! Rappaccini! and is *this* the upshot of your experiment!"

Related Readings

Caliban

by Norrie Epstein

In recent years, some scholars have started to rethink what Shakespeare might have intended in his depiction of Caliban, Prospero's slave. In the following essay, Norrie Epstein discusses these new interpretations.

Critics have recently taken a revisionist approach to *The Tempest,* seeing Caliban, not Prospero, as the play's real hero. If the play is interpreted as an indictment of colonialism, Prospero is the arrogant European adventurer who seizes another's land, imposing his culture and language on the natives who trust him. In this view, Prospero is not a wise ruler but a white dictator who tyrannizes his daughter, Caliban, and Ariel, and thus does to others what was done to him in Milan. Similar to the Native Americans, Caliban originally shows the new settlers where to collect berries and water—in short, he shows them how to survive in the new land. Only later does he plot the white man's destruction, not because he is innately evil but because he is enslaved on the land that is rightfully his own. Almost the first words Caliban speaks in the play claim his hereditary right to the island and his grievance against the man who has stolen it: "This island's mine, by Sycorax my mother, / Which thou tak'st from me" (I.2.332–33).

Shakespeare is typically ambiguous with regard to Caliban's character. Called a monster by the Europeans (who are too drunk to observe him), he is blessed with the loveliest and most tender lines in the play—lines that express his deep joy in the island that's no longer his:

> Be not afeared: the isle is full of noises,
> Sounds and sweet airs that give delight and hurt not.
> Sometimes a thousand twangling instruments
> Will hum about mine ears; and sometime voices
> That, if I then had waked after long sleep,
> Will make me sleep again; and then, in dreaming,
> The clouds methought would open and show riches
> Ready to drop upon me, that, when I waked,
> I cried to dream again.
> (III.2.132–44)

It's also intriguing that this illiterate brute utters verse when alone and prose when with Europeans.

Until recently Caliban had traditionally been played as either a fish, a lizard, an ape, a frog, or a monster with scales and fins—never a man. In 1978 David Suchet changed all that. Having been offered the role in the 1978–79 production of the Royal Shakespeare Company, Suchet, tired of the Caliban-as-monster portrayals, began to examine the text carefully, as well as accounts of discoveries in the New World published during Shakespeare's lifetime. The evidence for regarding Caliban as a beast is the drunken Trinculo's comment, "A fish: he smells like a fish . . . A strange fish . . . his fins like arms!" (II.2.25–34). Suchet writes: "Shakespeare did *not* write 'arms like fins.' And I started to read the speech again and it became so clear to me, that Shakespeare was not describing a fishlike man but a human being whose appearance, let alone his smell, was strange to Trinculo." Noting that native Africans and Americans had been often characterized by Europeans as monsters, Suchet concluded that in creating Caliban, Shakespeare was meticulously describing the popular misconception of an African or

American native, not an actual monster at all. Since the play has always been presented from Prospero's European perspective, audiences tend to sympathize with the learned magician, particularly when he exiles Caliban after the latter attempts to rape Miranda—an act that has always been an obstacle to identifying with Caliban. Suchet, however, sees the attempted rape as Caliban's natural desire to people his island with his own kind. In Act I, scene 2, he recalls his attempt and with surprising wit laughs, "O ho, O ho! Would't had been done! / Thou didst prevent me; I had peopled else / This isle with Calibans." Caliban's tragedy consists not only in the loss of his home but in his need for a master—whether the foolish Trinculo or the wise Prospero doesn't seem to matter. With *The Tempest,* Shakespeare gives us a strikingly accurate glimpse into the future of English imperialism, which was then in its early stages. As Joseph Conrad's *Heart of Darkness* and Rudyard Kipling's *The Man Who Would Be King* point out, greedy Europeans are only too eager to supply natives with gods.

It would be too facile to interpret *The Tempest* simply as a condemnation of colonialism. The play presents the problem from both perspectives—that of the colonists, who like Prospero were themselves exiles in search of a home; and that of the natives, like Caliban, exiled in their own country. Suchet's performance demonstrated that, as in the case of Shylock, Shakespeare reveals the humanity within the alien, showing us, if we let him, how to be humane. In "Mixed Blood: Columbus's Legacy," Richard Rodriguez writes: "European vocabularies do not have a silence rich enough to describe the force within Indian contemplation. Only Shakespeare, of all Europeans, understood that Indians have eyes. . . . Shakespeare saw Caliban eyeing his master's books, well, why not his master as well?"

Related Readings

from A Tempest

by Aimé Césaire

In the previous related reading, you learned that some people currently view Caliban as a symbol of colonized people everywhere. Contemporary playwright Aimé Cesaire also takes up the issue of colonialism in The Tempest *in his satirical play of the same name. In this excerpt, Prospero, Caliban, and Ariel get into a conversation that would have caused a furor in Shakespeare's time.*

(*Enter* Ariel.)
Prospero. Well, Ariel?
Ariel. Mission accomplished.
Prospero. Bravo; good work! But what seems to be the matter? I give you a compliment and you don't seem pleased? Are you tired?
Ariel. Not tired; disgusted. I obeyed you but—well, why not come out with it?—I did so most unwillingly. It was a real pity to see that great ship go down, so full of life.
Prospero. Oh, so you're upset, are you! It's always like that with you intellectuals! Who cares! What interests me is not your moods, but your deeds. Let's split: I'll take the zeal and you can keep your doubts. Agreed?
Ariel. Master, I must beg you to spare me this kind of labour.
Prospero (*shouting*). Listen, and listen good! There's a task to be performed, and I don't care how it gets done!
Ariel. You've promised me my freedom a thousand times, and I'm still waiting.

Prospero. Ingrate! And who freed you from Sycorax, may I ask? Who rent the pine in which you had been imprisoned and brought you forth?

Ariel. Sometimes I almost regret it . . . After all, I might have turned into a real tree in the end . . . Tree: that's a word that really gives me a thrill! It often springs to mind: palm tree—springing into the sky like a fountain ending in nonchalant, squid-like elegance. The baobab—twisted like the soft entrails of some monster. Ask the calao bird that lives a cloistered season in its branches. Or the Ceiba tree—spread out beneath the proud sun. O bird, o green mansions set in the living earth!

Prospero. Stuff it! I don't like talking trees. As for your freedom, you'll have it when I'm good and ready. In the meanwhile, see to the ship. I'm going to have a few words with Master Caliban. I've been keeping my eye on him, and he's getting a little too emancipated. *(calling)* Caliban! Caliban! *(He sighs.)*

Caliban. Uhuru!

Prospero. What did you say?

Caliban. I said, Uhuru!

Prospero. Mumbling your native language again! I've already told you, I don't like it. You could be polite, at least; a simple "hello" wouldn't kill you.

Caliban. Oh, I forgot . . . But make that as froggy, waspish, pustular and dung-filled "hello" as possible. May today hasten by a decade the day when all the birds of the sky and beasts of the earth will feast upon your corpse!

Prospero. Gracious as always, you ugly ape! How can anyone be so ugly?

Caliban. You think I'm ugly . . . well, I don't think you're so handsome yourself. With that big hooked nose, you look just like some old vulture. *(laughing)* An old vulture with a scrawny neck!

Prospero. Since you're so fond of invective, you

could at least thank me for having taught you to speak at all. You, a savage . . . a dumb animal, a beast I educated, trained, dragged up from the bestiality that still clings to you.

Caliban. In the first place, that's not true. You didn't teach me a thing! Except to jabber in your own language so that I could understand your orders: chop the wood, wash the dishes, fish for food, plant vegetables, all because you're too lazy to do it yourself. And as for your learning, did you ever impart any of *that* to me? No, you took care not to. All your science you keep for yourself alone, shut up in those big books.

Prospero. What would you be without me?

Caliban. Without you? I'd be the king, that's what I'd be, the King of the Island. The king of the island given me by my mother, Sycorax.

Prospero. There are some family trees it's better not to climb! She's a ghoul! A witch from whom—and may God be praised—death has delivered us.

Caliban. Dead or alive, she was my mother, and I won't deny her! Anyhow, you only think she's dead because you think the earth itself is dead . . . It's so much simpler that way! Dead, you can walk on it, pollute it, you can tread upon it with the steps of a conqueror. I respect the earth, because I know that it is alive, and I know that Sycorax is alive.

Sycorax. Mother.
Serpent, rain, lightning.
And I see thee everywhere!
In the eye of the stagnant pool which stares back at me,
through the rushes,
in the gesture made by twisted root and its awaiting thrust.
In the night, the all-seeing blinded night,
the nostril-less all-smelling night!

. . . Often, in my dreams, she speaks to me and warns me . . . Yesterday, even, when I was lying by the stream on my belly lapping at the muddy water, when the Beast was about to spring upon me with that huge stone in his hand . . .

Prospero. If you keep on like that even your magic won't save you from punishment!

Caliban. That's right, that's right! In the beginning, the gentleman was all sweet talk: dear Caliban here, my little Caliban there! And what do you think you'd have done without me in this strange land? Ingrate! I taught you the trees, fruits, birds, the seasons, and now you don't give a damn . . . Caliban the animal, Caliban the slave! I know that story! Once you've squeezed the juice from the orange, you toss the rind away!

Prospero. Oh!

Caliban. Do I lie? Isn't it true that you threw me out of your house and made me live in a filthy cave. The ghetto!

Prospero. It's easy to say "ghetto"! It wouldn't be such a ghetto if you took the trouble to keep it clean! And there's something you forgot, which is that what forced me to get rid of you was your lust. Good God, you tried to rape my daughter!

Caliban. Rape! Rape! Listen, you old goat, you're the one that put those dirty thoughts in my head. Let me tell you something: I couldn't care less about your daughter, or about your cave, for that matter. If I gripe, it's on principle, because I didn't like living with you at all, as a matter of fact.

Your feet stink!

Prospero. I did not summon you here to argue. Out! Back to work! Wood, water, and lots of both! I'm expecting company today.

Caliban. I've had just about enough. There's already a pile of wood that high . . .

Prospero. Enough! Careful, Caliban! If you keep grumbling you'll be whipped. And if you don't step lively, if you keep dragging your feet or try to strike or sabotage things, I'll beat you. Beating is the only language you really understand. So much the worse for you: I'll speak it, loud and clear. Get a move on!

Caliban. All right, I'm going . . . but this is the last time. It's the last time, do you hear me? Oh . . . I forgot: I've got something important to tell you.

Prospero. Important? Well, out with it.

Caliban. It's this: I've decided I don't want to be called Caliban any longer.

Prospero. What kind of rot is that? I don't understand.

Caliban. Put it this way: I'm *telling* you that from now on I won't answer to the name Caliban.

Prospero. Where did you get that idea?

Caliban. Well, because Caliban *isn't* my name. It's as simple as that.

Prospero. Oh, I suppose it's mine!

Caliban. It's the name given me by your hatred, and every time it's spoken it's an insult.

Prospero. My, aren't we getting sensitive! All right, suggest something else . . . I've got to call you something. What will it be? Cannibal would suit you, but I'm sure you wouldn't like that, would you? Let's see . . . what about Hannibal? That fits. And why not . . . they all seem to like historical names.

Caliban. Call me X. That would be best. Like a man without a name. Or, to be more precise, a man whose name has been stolen. You talk about history . . . well, that's history, and everyone knows it! Every time you summon me it reminds me of a basic fact, the fact that you've stolen everything from me, even my identity! Uhuru! *(He exits.)*

(Enter Ariel as a sea-nymph.)

Prospero. My dear Ariel, did you see how he looked

from *A Tempest*

at me, that glint in his eye? That's something new. Well, let me tell you, Caliban is the enemy. As for those people on the boat, I've changed my mind about them. Give them a scare, but for God's sake don't touch a hair of their heads! You'll answer to me if you do.

Ariel. I've suffered too much myself for having made them suffer not to be pleased at your mercy. You can count on me, Master.

Prospero. Yes, however great their crimes, if they repent you can assure them of my forgiveness. They are men of my race, and of high rank. As for me, at my age one must rise above disputes and quarrels and think about the future. I have a daughter. Alonso has a son. If they were to fall in love, I would give my consent. Let Ferdinand marry Miranda, and may their marriage bring us harmony and peace. That is my plan. I want it executed. As for Caliban, does it matter what that villain plots against me? All the nobility of Italy, Naples and Milan henceforth combined, will protect me bodily. Go!

Ariel. Yes, Master. Your orders will be fully carried out.

Related Readings

I Will Come Back

by Pablo Neruda

At the end of the play, as Prospero leaves the magical island that has been his home for so many years, perhaps he would have expressed the same heart-felt sentiments as the speaker of this poem.

Some time, man or woman, traveller,
afterwards, when I am not alive,
look here, look for me here
between the stones and the ocean,
in the light storming
in the foam.
Look here, look for me here,
for here is where I shall come, saying nothing,
no voice, no mouth, pure,
here I shall be again the movement
of the water, of
its wild heart,
here I shall be both lost and found—
here I shall be perhaps both stone and silence.

—*Translated by Alistair Reid*